D0332758

easy everyday

simple recipes for no-fuss food

RYLAND
PETERS
& SMALL

LONDON NEW YORK

Senior Designer Toni Kay

Editor Céline Hughes

Picture Research Emily Westlake

Production Toby Marshall

Art Director Leslie Harrington

Publishing Director Alison Starling

Indexer Penelope Kent

First published in the United Kingdom
in 2008 by Ryland Peters & Small
20–21 Jockey's Fields
London WC1R 4BW
www.rylandpeters.com

10 9 8 7 6 5 4 3 2

Text © Ghillie Basan, Fiona Beckett,
Susannah Blake, Tamsin Burnett-Hall,
Maxine Clark, Linda Collister,
Tonia George, Brian Glover,
Rachael Anne Hill, Jennifer Joyce,
Caroline Marson, Jane Noraika,
Louise Pickford, Jennie Shapter,
Sonia Stevenson, Linda Tubby,
Fran Warde, Laura Washburn and
Ryland Peters & Small 2008

Design and photographs
© Ryland Peters & Small 2008

ISBN: 978-1-84597-633-0

The recipes in this book have been
published previously by Ryland Peters
& Small.

The authors' moral rights have
been asserted. All rights reserved.
No part of this publication may
be reproduced, stored in a retrieval
system or transmitted in any form or
by any means, electronic, mechanical,
photocopying or otherwise, without
the prior permission of the publisher.

A CIP record for this book is available
from the British Library.

Printed and bound in China

Notes:

• All spoon measurements are level, unless otherwise specified.

• Ovens should be preheated to the specified temperature.
Recipes in this book were tested using a regular oven. If using
a fan-assisted oven, follow the manufacturer's instructions for
adjusting temperatures.

• All eggs are medium, unless otherwise specified. Recipes
containing raw or partially cooked egg, or raw fish or shellfish,
should not be served to the very young, very old, anyone with
a compromised immune system or pregnant women.

easy everyday

CONTENTS

When you've had a busy day or you've just come home from work, the last thing you want to do is spend your evening in the kitchen cooking up a storm. Although it's all too tempting to buy a ready-meal on the way home or order in a takeaway, nothing beats a freshly made, home-cooked meal. Flick through *Easy Everyday* and you will find plenty of delicious, easy recipes to inspire you whether you are feeding a whole hungry family or just one other person. And with all sorts of dishes, from soups and quick snacks to hearty mains and scrumptious desserts, there's an idea here for every occasion.

You don't have to scour the supermarket for obscure ingredients or slave over a hot stove for hours to make the recipes in this book. Every one is designed to be simple, satisfying and hassle-free – perfect for every day. Some are super quick for when the family's clamouring for their dinner; others require minimum preparation followed by an hour or so in the oven so that you can get on with your evening while supper's cooking.

You won't just have the evening meal covered with *Easy Everyday* – there are salads and lunchboxes to help you make lunches that both you and the children will love. And the chapter on drinks lets you try some fresh, healthy herbal teas, juices and smoothies.

Everyone can make easy everyday food with the help of these fantastic recipes. Tuck in and try one today.

INTRODUCTION

SOUPS

This marvellous dish is aromatherapy in a soup. Purée it coarsely, so the brilliant carrot orange is just flecked with green. The bocconcini – *little mouthfuls of mini-mozzarellas – peep out from just under the surface. Sprinkle with Chinese flowering chives if you can find them, otherwise regular chives are just fine.*

3 thin leeks, thinly sliced

2 garlic cloves, crushed

1 tablespoon sunflower oil

600 g young carrots, well scrubbed and thinly sliced

1.2 litres vegetable stock or water

40 g fresh sorrel, stalks removed and leaves chopped

leaves from 4 fresh tarragon sprigs

leaves from 6 fresh parsley sprigs

leaves from 4 fresh basil sprigs

leaves from 6 fresh marjoram sprigs

TO SERVE

100 ml crème fraîche

12 bocconcini, torn in half, or 2 mozzarellas, torn into pieces

a handful of Chinese flowering chives (kuchai), or regular chives

freshly ground black pepper

SERVES 6

herb and carrot soup

Put the leeks, garlic and oil in a small saucepan, cover with a lid and cook gently for 5 minutes. Add the carrots and cook gently for a further 5 minutes. Add the stock or water, bring to the boil and simmer for 5 minutes. Lower the heat, add the sorrel and simmer, uncovered, for a further 5 minutes.

Coarsely chop the tarragon, parsley, basil and marjoram. Stir into the soup. Strain the mixture through a sieve into a clean pan and put the solids into a food processor or blender with a little of the liquid. Blend to a coarse purée, then return to the pan and reheat.

Remove from the heat and fold in the crème fraîche. Ladle into hot bowls and add a few *bocconcini* pieces to each one. Sprinkle with chive flowers or regular chives and pepper, then serve.

An old-fashioned, nourishing soup, full of healthy green things. If you cannot find sorrel in your local supermarket, it can be omitted.

kitchen garden soup

1 fresh bay leaf

1 small cabbage, quartered

60 g unsalted butter

2 leeks, halved and sliced

1 onion, chopped

2 teaspoons salt

250 g new potatoes, chopped

a handful of fresh flat leaf parsley, chopped

250 g fresh shelled peas

1 Little Gem lettuce, quartered and sliced thinly

a handful of fresh sorrel, sliced

sea salt and freshly ground black pepper

unsalted butter and/or crème fraîche, to serve (optional)

SERVES 4–6

Put the bay leaf in a large saucepan of water and bring to the boil. Add the cabbage quarters and blanch for 3 minutes. Drain the cabbage, pat dry and slice thinly.

Heat the butter in a large saucepan. Add the cabbage, leeks, onion and 2 teaspoons salt and cook until softened, 5–10 minutes. Add the potatoes, parsley and 2 litres water. Season to taste and simmer gently for 40 minutes.

Stir in the peas, lettuce and sorrel and cook for 10 minutes more. Taste for seasoning. Ladle into bowls, add 1 tablespoon butter and/or crème fraîche, if using, to each and serve.

golden butternut squash soup

1 kg butternut squash, peeled

2 tablespoons olive oil

2 onions, diced

1 garlic clove, crushed

1.2 litres chicken or
vegetable stock

sea salt and freshly ground
black pepper

single cream, to serve (optional)

SERVES 4

*Squash is a wonderfully versatile vegetable, and
it's used to great effect in this flavoursome soup.*

Cut the squash in half lengthways and use a spoon to scoop
out the seeds. Chop the flesh into 2-cm pieces.

Heat the oil in a large saucepan, add the squash, onions and
garlic and sauté over low heat for 10 minutes. Add the stock,
bring to the boil, then simmer for 30 minutes.

Using a hand-held blender, blitz the soup until smooth and
creamy. Season and serve with a drizzle of cream, if liked.

flag bean soup

1 tablespoon olive oil, plus extra to taste

3 large garlic cloves: 2 cut into slices and 1 crushed

1 large onion, finely chopped

250 g Puy lentils, rinsed

1 litre boiling chicken or vegetable stock, plus extra to taste

100 g tinned butter beans

200 g tinned green flageolet beans

200 g tinned red kidney beans

200 g tinned haricot or cannellini beans

sea salt and freshly ground black pepper

TO SERVE

fresh parsley or basil leaves

basil oil or olive oil, to drizzle

grated lemon zest (optional)

crusty bread

SERVES 4

This flag bean soup is so-called because the beans are red, green and white, the colour of the Italian flag. It's exactly the sort of soup you need on a cold winter's day. Using tinned beans, it takes no time at all to prepare, and you can use vegetable or chicken stock to suit either vegetarians or meat-eaters.

Heat the olive oil in a frying pan, add the sliced garlic and fry gently on both sides until crisp and golden. Remove and drain on kitchen paper.

Put the onion and crushed garlic in the frying pan, adding extra oil if necessary, and cook gently until softened and transparent. Add the lentils and half the stock and cook until the lentils are just tender.

Meanwhile, rinse and drain all the beans. Put them in a sieve and dunk the sieve in a large saucepan of boiling water. The beans are cooked – you are just reheating them.

Add the hot beans to the lentils and add the remaining stock. Taste, and add salt and pepper as necessary. If the soup is too thick, add extra boiling stock or water. Ladle into bowls, top with the reserved fried garlic and the herbs, drizzle with a few drops of basil oil and top with lemon zest, if using. Serve with crusty bread.

The tastiest meals are often the very simplest. To make truly wholesome tomato soup, all you need is fresh tomato sauce, thinned down with stock, heated until almost but not quite boiling (otherwise it loses its fresh taste), then finished off with lemon juice and zest and a spoonful of pesto.

tomato soup

1 kg very ripe red tomatoes

500 ml chicken stock, or to taste

sea salt and coarsely crushed black pepper

grated zest and freshly squeezed juice of 1 unwaxed lemon

4 tablespoons pesto, to serve

SERVES 4

To skin the tomatoes, cut a cross in the base of each and dunk into a saucepan of boiling water. Remove after 10 seconds and transfer to a sieve set over a large saucepan. Slip off and discard the skins and cut the tomatoes in half around their 'equators'. Using a teaspoon, deseed into the sieve, then press the pulp and juice through the sieve and add to a blender. Discard the seeds. Chop the tomato halves and add to the blender. Alternatively, put through a mouli food mill.

Purée the tomatoes, adding a little of the stock to help the process – you may have to work in batches. Add the remaining stock, season to taste and transfer to the saucepan. Heat well without boiling. Serve in heated soup plates topped with a spoonful of lemon juice, pesto, lemon zest and pepper.

cream of broccoli soup
with leeks and broad beans

2 large leeks, halved and sliced

2 tablespoons butter

2 tablespoons sunflower oil

2 large heads broccoli, broken into florets

1 medium baking potato, chopped

600 ml vegetable or chicken stock

250 g shelled broad beans, fresh or frozen

sea salt and freshly ground white pepper

basil or parsley oil, to serve

SERVES 4

A pale green, fresh, summery soup that can be adapted to other ingredients – it's also good with cauliflower and cannellini beans, or sweet potatoes and fresh borlottis. Feel free to use frozen broad beans. Like peas and corn, they are one of the few ingredients that can be better frozen. Picked and frozen almost immediately, their sugars have no time to turn to starch.

Put the butter and oil in a large saucepan and heat until the butter melts. Add the leeks and fry gently until softened but not browned. Reserve a few spoonfuls of the cooked leeks for garnish.

Add the broccoli to the pan and stir-fry until bright green. Add the potato and stock and bring to the boil. Reduce the heat, season and simmer for 30 minutes, topping up with boiling water if necessary.

If using frozen broad beans, cook in boiling salted water until just tender, then drain and transfer to a bowl of cold water. Pop the cooked beans out of their grey skins and discard the skins – the bright green beans look and taste better. Reserve a few spoonfuls of broad beans for serving.

Strain the soup into a bowl and put the solids and remaining broad beans in a blender or food processor. Add 2 ladles of the strained liquid and purée until smooth. Add the remaining liquid and blend again. If the soup is too thick, thin it with water. Reheat the soup, pour into heated soup bowls, top with the reserved leeks and skinned broad beans, then serve with a trickle of basil or parsley oil over the top.

soupe au pistou

4 tablespoons olive oil

1 red onion, cut into wedges

1 large potato,
cut into 1-cm cubes

a handful (about 125 g) of soup
pasta, such as orecchiette (or the
traditional vermicelli)

1 litre chicken or vegetable stock

250 g cooked or tinned cannellini
beans, rinsed and drained

4 baby carrots, halved or
quartered lengthways

250 g Brussels sprouts, halved,
or baby courgettes,
cut into thick slices

1 red pepper, peeled, cored
and sliced

250 g fresh shelled peas

sea salt and freshly ground
black pepper

PISTOU

leaves from a handful of fresh basil

2 garlic cloves, crushed

olive oil (see method)

SERVES 4

Pistou is the Provençal version of pesto, and to make it you need a big bunch of scented summertime basil. Unlike pesto, it doesn't contain pine nuts or cheese. This version of the soup is quicker to cook than the traditional one. If you'd like the classic, cook it all together – beans first; then root vegetables and pasta; then fresh peas, followed by leafy things. Red kidney beans are often included, but this version uses white beans instead.

To make the *pistou*, put the basil and garlic in a blender or food processor and blend as finely as possible. Add enough olive oil in a steady stream to form a loose paste. Set aside.

Heat the oil in a small frying pan, add the onion wedges and fry gently on both sides until softened. Cook the potato and soup pasta in salted boiling water until tender. Drain. Blanch your choice of carrots, sprouts, courgettes, pepper and peas, in salted boiling water until tender but crisp, about 3–5 minutes. Drain and refresh in cold water.

Bring the stock to the boil and add the seasoning, pasta and all the vegetables including the cannellini beans. Simmer for 2 minutes or until heated through.

Serve in heated soup plates, with a separate bowl of *pistou*. Let people stir the *pistou* into their own soup to taste.

alphabet soup

100 g smoked pancetta, cubed

1 tablespoon olive oil

½ onion, chopped

1 large potato, cubed and rinsed

1 carrot, quartered lengthways, then sliced crossways into triangles

2 celery sticks, sliced

2 small courgettes, quartered lengthways, then sliced crossways into triangles

3 tomatoes, halved, deseeded and chopped

1 litre chicken stock

500 g alfabetto soup pasta

½ small round cabbage, quartered, cored and sliced

100 g green beans, cut into 2-cm lengths

100 g peas, fresh or frozen

about 200 g tinned beans, such as cannellini, red kidney or chickpeas, rinsed and drained

sea salt and freshly ground black pepper

TO SERVE

2 tablespoons freshly chopped parsley

crusty Italian bread

freshly grated Cheddar

SERVES 4

Beloved of children everywhere, alphabet pasta can be added to all sorts of other soups, but is especially useful with vegetable soups, to encourage little ones to eat their greens. The bacon and chicken stock make the soup flavoursome, but if you would like to stay vegetarian, use a well-flavoured vegetable stock and a few spoonfuls of crushed tomatoes.

Put the pancetta in a stockpot, heat gently and fry until the fat runs. Add the olive oil, heat briefly, then add the onion and cook gently until softened but not browned.

Add the potato, carrot, celery, courgettes, tomatoes and some seasoning. Add the stock and pasta and heat until simmering. Cook over low heat for about 15 minutes. Add the cabbage and beans, bring to the boil and cook for 5 minutes, then add the peas and tinned beans and cook for another 2–3 minutes until all the vegetables are tender. Season to taste, sprinkle with parsley, then serve with bread and cheese (shown here melted on top of the bread).

japanese fresh corn soup
with spring onions and soy sauce

4 ears of fresh corn or about 500 g fresh corn kernels

1 litre hot chicken stock

4 egg yolks

4 spring onions, sliced diagonally

2 tablespoons dark soy sauce

cracked pepper, or a Japanese pepper mixture, such as furikake seasoning or seven-spice

SERVES 4

This is a variation on a traditional Japanese summer soup, prized for the fresh taste of corn – and very easy to make.

Bring a large saucepan of water to the boil, add the corn and simmer for about 2 minutes. Drain. Hold the corn upright on a chopping board, blunt end down. Run a sharp knife down the cobs, shaving off the kernels. Reserve a few sliced-off sections of kernels for serving, blanching them in boiling water for 2 minutes.

Put the remaining kernels in a blender with 250 ml of the stock. Purée until smooth, then press through a sieve into a saucepan. Return the corn to the blender, add another ladle of stock, purée, then strain as before, pushing through as much corn juice as possible. Repeat until all the stock has been used. Reheat the mixture, then remove from the heat.

Put 1 egg yolk into each of 4 small soup bowls, ladle the soup on top and beat with chopsticks (the hot soup cooks the egg). Alternatively, whisk all 4 egg yolks in a mixing bowl, beat into the soup, then ladle into bowls. Serve, topped with spring onions, the reserved kernel sections, soy sauce and pepper to taste.

laksa

3 tablespoons peanut oil

500 ml tinned coconut milk

2 boneless chicken breasts, skinned and thickly sliced

fish sauce or salt, to taste

750 g fresh or 100 g dried udon noodles

SPICE PASTE

3–6 red or orange chillies, cored and chopped

1 shallot, chopped

2 lemongrass stalks, finely sliced

3 cm fresh ginger, finely sliced

½ teaspoon ground turmeric

6 blanched almonds, chopped

1 tablespoon fish sauce or a pinch of salt

1 garlic clove, crushed

TO SERVE

1 packet fresh beansprouts, trimmed, rinsed and drained

4 spring onions, sliced diagonally

1 red chilli, cored and finely sliced

fresh coriander (optional)

SERVES 4

Laksas are spicy soups from Malaysia, Indonesia and the Philippines, though the Malay ones are the best known. They generally contain vegetables, prawns, pork and noodles, but this varies from region to region. This one contains chicken, but feel free to use fish or other seafood instead. The spice paste is the key – usually laboriously made with a mortar and pestle, a blender is an easy, modern alternative.

Put all the spice paste ingredients into a spice grinder or blender and work to a paste (add a little water if necessary).

Heat the oil in a wok, add the spice paste and cook gently for about 5 minutes until aromatic. Add the thick part of the coconut milk (if any) and stir-fry until it releases its oil, then add the thinner part and heat gently. Add 1 litre water and bring to the boil. Add the chicken, reduce the heat and poach gently without boiling until the meat is cooked through, about 10–15 minutes. Add the fish sauce or salt, to taste.

If using fresh noodles, rinse in cold water, then boil for about 1–2 minutes. If using dried noodles, cook in unsalted boiling water for 3–5 minutes, or until done, then drain. Divide the noodles between large soup bowls. Add the chicken and liquid, top with the beansprouts, spring onions, chilli and coriander, if using, and serve.

This super-healthy chunky soup is full of interesting flavours. Lentils give the soup colour and texture, but they also pack a powerful protein punch while helping to reduce cholesterol.

smoked haddock and puy lentil chowder

100 g Puy lentils, rinsed

2 leeks, rinsed and chopped

600 ml vegetable, fish or chicken stock

8 small new potatoes, scrubbed and diced

300 ml skimmed milk

350 g smoked haddock fillets, skinned

sea salt and freshly ground black pepper

2 tablespoons scissor-snipped fresh chives, to serve

SERVES 4

Put the rinsed lentils in a saucepan, add enough boiling water to cover the lentils by 4 cm, cover the saucepan and simmer for 15–20 minutes until tender, then drain.

Meanwhile, simmer the leeks in 4 tablespoons of the stock in a large saucepan, covered, for 3–4 minutes until softened. Stir in the potatoes, milk and remaining stock. Season and bring to the boil, then simmer for 15 minutes or until the potatoes are tender.

Add the smoked haddock to the saucepan and simmer for 4–5 minutes until the fish flakes easily. Lift the haddock out of the pan and break into large flakes.

Stir the lentils into the chowder, ladle into bowls and top with the flaked smoked haddock. Add a scattering of chives and serve.

chicken soup

1 tablespoon olive oil

1 onion, chopped

1 garlic clove, crushed

2 chicken breasts, diced

2 leeks, chopped

200 g potatoes, unpeeled and chopped

1.2 litres chicken stock

3 fresh thyme sprigs

2 bay leaves

kernels from 1 cob of sweetcorn

sea salt and freshly ground black pepper

SERVES 4

A bowlful of this comforting soup makes everyone feel better, especially when served with a slab of warm crusty bread.

Heat the olive oil in a saucepan, add the onion, garlic, chicken and leeks and sauté gently for 8 minutes without browning. Add the potatoes, stock, thyme and bay leaves, then season and simmer for 20 minutes.

Add the sweetcorn kernels and cook for a further 10 minutes. Remove the thyme and bay leaves before serving.

sausage soup

16 thin pork sausages, pricked with a fork

3 onions, chopped

3 tomatoes, skinned (see page 19), deseeded and chopped

olive oil, to sprinkle

250 g smoked pancetta or streaky bacon, coarsely chopped

2 garlic cloves, crushed with a pinch of salt

a large fresh sage sprig, sliced

1 baguette, sliced

250 g cheese, such as Cheddar, coarsely grated

sea salt and freshly ground black pepper

freshly chopped parsley, to serve (optional)

SERVES 4

Here's a deliciously satisfying soup from the south of France. It serves four as a simple winter supper, but it can easily be made more substantial by adding the suggestions in the note below.

Preheat the oven to 200°C (400°F) Gas 6.

Arrange the sausages in a ring around a large, shallow, flameproof casserole dish or baking dish. Put the onions and tomatoes in the middle and sprinkle with olive oil. Cook in the preheated oven until done (about 30 minutes, depending on the thickness of the sausages). Stir the onions and tomatoes after 15–20 minutes to stop them burning. Leave the oven on.

When the sausages are done, remove, cut into 3–4 pieces each and set aside. Put the dish on top of the stove and add the pancetta or bacon. Fry, stirring, until crisp, and the fat is starting to run. Add the garlic and fry for about 1 minute, then add the sage. Add about 1 litre water and stir. Taste and adjust the seasoning, adding extra water if the mixture is too thick.

Meanwhile, put the slices of baguette on a baking sheet and cook at the top of the oven until golden. Remove from the oven and sprinkle with grated cheese. Return to the oven until the cheese has melted and become almost crisp. To serve, put about 3 cheese-topped croutes in 4 soup plates, ladle in the soup and top with the sausages. Sprinkle with parsley, if using, and serve.

Notes

• If you like, serve the croutes separately. Adding them at the end keeps them crisp to the last possible moment, though the method of pouring the soup over them is traditionally French.

• The pancetta may be omitted, but the soup will need more seasoning. Other vegetables such as quartered and sliced courgettes or cabbage may also be used.

It seems that most dishes containing chorizo taste pretty good. This soup is no exception and needs no embellishments, making it refreshingly simple to prepare. Make sure you buy the correct chorizo – you want the short, fat, little cured sausages. They are ready to eat but are so much better when they are fried and crispy.

chickpea, tomato and chorizo soup

200 g chorizo, roughly chopped

1 red onion, chopped

2 garlic cloves, crushed

a 400-g tin chopped plum tomatoes

2 fresh thyme sprigs

a 400-g tin chickpeas, drained and rinsed

1 litre vegetable stock

sea salt and freshly ground black pepper

SERVES 4

Put the chorizo in a large saucepan or casserole dish over medium heat and cook until it starts to release its oil. Continue to cook, stirring, for 4–5 minutes until it is lovely and crisp.

Add the red onion and garlic and turn the heat right down to allow them to soften in the chorizo's paprika-infused oil. After 6–7 minutes the onion and garlic should be translucent and glossy. Add the tomatoes and thyme and turn the heat back up. Cook for 5 minutes to intensify the flavour, then add the chickpeas and stock. Return to the boil, cover and simmer for 15 minutes.

Remove the thyme. Season well and simmer for a further 10 minutes to allow all the flavours to get to know one another.

Transfer to bowls and serve.

LUNCHBOXES & SALADS

The spices and flavourings used in this recipe are typical of North African cooking, and all over the region, pita bread is stuffed with grilled meat, salad and yoghurt. Use other minced meats if you prefer.

lamb in pita bread

2 teaspoons coriander seeds

1 teaspoon cumin seeds

2 tablespoons extra virgin olive oil

1 onion, finely chopped

2 garlic cloves, crushed

1 teaspoon ground cinnamon

1/4–1/2 teaspoon cayenne pepper

300 g minced lamb

a pinch of salt

2 tablespoons freshly chopped coriander leaves

4 pita breads

a few salad leaves, such as cos lettuce and watercress

plain yoghurt or tahini sauce

1 tablespoon sesame seeds, toasted in a dry frying pan

SERVES 4

Put the coriander seeds and cumin seeds into a small dry frying pan and fry until they start to brown and release their aroma. Leave to cool slightly, then grind to powder in a spice grinder (use a clean coffee grinder) or with a mortar and pestle.

Heat the oil in a frying pan, add the onion, garlic, ground coriander, cumin and cinnamon, and the pepper and fry gently for 5 minutes until softened but not golden. Increase the heat, add the lamb and the pinch of salt and stir-fry for 5–8 minutes until well browned. Stir in the fresh coriander.

Meanwhile, lightly toast the pita bread and cut a long slit in the side of each one. Carefully fill with a few salad leaves, add the minced lamb mixture, a spoonful of yoghurt or tahini and sprinkle with sesame seeds. Serve hot.

The hoummus in these wraps is a great source of monounsaturated fat – the sort that not only lowers your bad cholesterol, but also maintains and may even increase your good cholesterol. The wraps are a doddle to make so they're great for putting together first thing in the morning before you leave the house.

2 tablespoons hoummus

4 small tortillas

1 large grilled chicken breast, cut into thin strips

½ small cucumber, cut into thin strips

4 medium cos or romaine lettuce leaves, shredded

4 teaspoons chilli oil or sweet chilli sauce

sea salt and freshly ground black pepper

4 cocktail sticks

SERVES 2

chicken and hoummus wraps

Spread ½ tablespoon hoummus over each tortilla. Put the strips of chicken and cucumber on top of the hoummus, then top with the shredded lettuce.

Drizzle each wrap with 1 teaspoon chilli oil or sweet chilli sauce and season generously. Carefully roll up the tortillas and secure each one in place with a cocktail stick. Chill the wraps in the refrigerator until you are ready to eat.

Variation If you prefer a vegetarian alternative, use tomato slices and rocket leaves instead of the chicken.

simple vegetable quiche

1 shop-bought wholemeal
pastry case

FILLING

100 g broccoli,
divided into small florets

1 tablespoon olive oil

1 onion, finely chopped

1 small red pepper,
sliced into rings and deseeded

1 carrot, about 75 g, grated

3 eggs

150 ml milk

¼ teaspoon freshly grated nutmeg

freshly ground black pepper,
to serve (optional)

SERVES 6–8

Kids love quiche and this meat-free version is a great way to increase your child's vegetable intake. Almost any vegetables can be used, so be creative. Ready-made pastry cases are available from health food stores. The finished quiche can be frozen for up to 1 month.

Preheat the oven to 200°C (400°F) Gas 6. Unwrap the pastry case and put it on a baking sheet.

Steam the broccoli florets over a saucepan of gently simmering water for 3 minutes. Plunge them into cold water and drain well.

Heat the oil in a non-stick frying pan, add the onion and fry gently for 5 minutes, stirring frequently. Transfer the onion to the pastry case, spreading it evenly over the base. Arrange the broccoli, pepper and carrot on top of the onion. Put the eggs, milk, nutmeg and black pepper in a bowl and beat well. Pour the mixture over the vegetables in the pastry case.

Bake in the preheated oven for 15 minutes. Reduce the temperature to 180°C (350°F) Gas 4 and continue to bake for about 20 minutes until the filling is set.

Variations

• Sprinkle the quiche with a little grated cheese just before baking.

• Add 1 tablespoon tinned cannellini beans to the filling.

• Replace the broccoli and carrot with about 200 g finely chopped, well drained, blanched spinach and 75 g crumbled goats' cheese.

double-decker bacon and turkey club sandwich

12 thick slices of white bread

4 tablespoons mayonnaise

8 slices of deli turkey

4 crisp leaves of butter lettuce

1 avocado, stoned, peeled and thinly sliced

8 paper-thin red onion slices

8 grilled, crispy, dry-cured bacon rashers

4 slices of beefsteak tomato

16 cocktail sticks

SERVES 4

The club is the ultimate sandwich; a toasted bread tower generously layered with meat, vegetables, and sometimes cheese. A truly special lunchtime treat.

Toast the bread, then spread one side of each piece of toast with the mayonnaise. Stack the turkey, lettuce and avocado on 4 of these and top with another piece of toast.

Stack the red onion, bacon and tomato over and top with the remaining toast. Cut the sandwich in half diagonally and then again diagonally in the opposite direction. Secure each quarter with a cocktail stick. Repeat with the other 3 sandwiches.

Baby spinach is essential for this recipe because the leaves wilt and soften quickly, so you needn't remove the stalks or chop the leaves. The pancetta adds a special depth of flavour. Like all frittatas, this one is wonderful for both picnics and packed lunches.

spinach and pancetta frittata

6 large eggs

1 tablespoon extra virgin olive or sunflower oil

125 g smoked pancetta, cubed, or smoked bacon lardons

4 spring onions, chopped

1 garlic clove, finely chopped

175 g baby spinach

sea salt and freshly ground black pepper

a 24-cm heavy frying pan (measure the base, not the top)

SERVES 4

Preheat the grill to medium.

Break the eggs into a bowl and whisk briefly with a fork. Season well.

Heat 1 tablespoon of the oil in the frying pan. Add the pancetta or bacon pieces and cook over medium heat for 3–4 minutes until they start to brown.

Add the spring onions, garlic and spinach and stir-fry for 3–4 minutes or until the spinach has wilted and the onions have softened.

Pour the egg mixture into the pan, quickly mix into the other ingredients and stop stirring. Reduce to a low heat and cook for 8–10 minutes, or until the top is almost set. Slide under the preheated grill to finish cooking the top. Cut into wedges and serve hot or cold.

A robust omelette packed full of goodness, this is a perfect recipe for using up small quantities of leftover vegetables, including ingredients such as broccoli, corn, broad beans or mushrooms. This tortilla is best finished under the grill to retain the lovely colours on the top when serving, but you can also turn it over in the pan to finish cooking in the classic way.

hearty country-style tortilla

4 tablespoons extra virgin olive or sunflower oil

3 medium potatoes, about 325 g, peeled and cubed

1 onion, halved and sliced

75 g green beans, trimmed and cut into three

4 asparagus spears, cut into 5-cm lengths

1 red pepper, quartered, deseeded and thinly sliced

75 g spicy chorizo, sliced

1 garlic clove, finely chopped

6 large eggs

75 g frozen peas

sea salt and freshly ground black pepper

a 24-cm heavy non-stick frying pan (measure the base, not the top)

SERVES 4–6

Preheat the grill to medium.

Heat 2 tablespoons of the oil in the frying pan. Add the potatoes and cook over medium heat for 5 minutes. Add the onion and cook for 10 minutes or until the potatoes are almost tender, lifting and turning occasionally.

Meanwhile put the beans and asparagus in a saucepan of salted boiling water and cook for 5 minutes. Drain and refresh in cold water. Drain well.

Add the pepper, chorizo, asparagus, beans and garlic to the potatoes and cook for 5 minutes, stirring frequently.

Break the eggs into a large bowl, season and whisk briefly with a fork. Mix in the peas and cooked vegetable mixture.

If necessary, wipe out the frying pan with kitchen paper, then add the remaining oil and heat until hot. Add the tortilla mixture, letting it spread evenly in the pan.

Cook over medium-low heat for about 10 minutes until the bottom is golden brown and the top almost set. Slide under the preheated grill to set and lightly brown the top. Transfer to a serving plate, cut into wedges and serve hot or warm.

tortilla with artichokes and serrano ham

3 tablespoons extra virgin olive
or sunflower oil

3 medium potatoes, about 350 g,
peeled and cubed

1 Spanish onion, chopped

5 large eggs

400 g tinned artichoke hearts in
water, well drained and halved

2 tablespoons fresh thyme leaves

100 g thinly sliced serrano ham,
torn into strips

6–8 slices goats' cheese log with
rind, about 125 g (optional)

sea salt and freshly ground
black pepper

a 24-cm heavy non-stick frying pan
(measure the base, not the top)

SERVES 3–4

Most tortillas are inverted onto a plate and returned to the pan to finish cooking. However, this tortilla is topped with cured mountain ham and should be finished under the grill. For a truly extravagant touch, add a few slices of goats' cheese log such as Soignon Petite Sainte-Maure, which melts beautifully into the top of the tortilla.

Preheat the grill to medium.

Heat 2 tablespoons of the oil in the frying pan. Add the potatoes and cook over medium heat for 5 minutes. Add the onion and cook for a further 10 minutes, lifting and turning occasionally, until just tender. The potatoes and onions should not brown very much.

Meanwhile, break the eggs into a large bowl, season and whisk briefly with a fork.

Add the artichokes, thyme and about three-quarters of the ham to the bowl of eggs. Add the potatoes and onion and stir gently.

Heat the remaining oil in the frying pan. Add the tortilla mixture, spreading it evenly in the pan. Cook over medium-low heat for about 6 minutes, then top with the remaining ham. Cook for a further 4–5 minutes or until the bottom is golden brown and the top almost set.

Add the goats' cheese, if using, and slide under the preheated grill just to brown the top, about 2–3 minutes. Cut into wedges and serve hot or warm.

saffron potato salad with sun-dried tomatoes and caper and basil dressing

500 g large, waxy, yellow-fleshed
potatoes, peeled

a pinch of saffron threads,
about 20

8 sun-dried tomatoes
(the dry kind, not in oil)

CAPER AND BASIL DRESSING

6 tablespoons extra virgin olive oil

3 tablespoons freshly chopped basil
leaves, plus extra to serve

2 tablespoons salted capers, rinsed
and chopped, if large

1–2 tablespoons freshly squeezed
lemon juice, to taste

sea salt and freshly ground
black pepper

SERVES 4

The potatoes absorb the glorious golden colour and subtle flavour of the saffron as they simmer gently with the tomatoes. The sunny colours of this salad are beautiful – yellow from the saffron, red from the tomato and green from the basil. If you can, serve this warm, as the heat will release the heady aromas of the basil and saffron.

Cut the potatoes into large chunks. Put in a saucepan, add enough cold water to just cover them, then add the saffron and sun-dried tomatoes. Bring slowly to the boil, then turn down the heat, cover and simmer very gently for about 12 minutes until just tender. If the water boils too fast, the potatoes will start to disintegrate. Drain well.

Pick out the now plumped up sun-dried tomatoes and slice them thinly. Tip the potatoes into a large bowl and add the sliced tomatoes.

To make the dressing, put the oil, chopped basil and capers in a small bowl. Add lemon juice and seasoning and mix well. Pour over the hot potatoes, mix gently, then serve hot or warm, scattered with extra basil leaves.

Puy lentils are a must here as they do not collapse when cooked. They make the salad filling and give it plenty of texture. You couldn't find an easier recipe.

300 g Puy lentils, rinsed

250 g cherry tomatoes

80 g stoned olives

75 g Parmesan

2 tablespoons balsamic vinegar

sea salt and freshly ground black pepper

olive oil, for baking and dressing

SERVES 4

lentil and baked tomato salad

Preheat the oven to 130°C (250°F) Gas 1.

Put the lentils in a saucepan, cover with water and bring to the boil. Lower the heat and simmer for 40 minutes, until soft.

Put the tomatoes on a non-stick baking sheet, drizzle 3 tablespoons olive oil over them, then bake in the preheated oven for 40 minutes.

Drain the lentils when cooked and put in a serving bowl. Add the tomatoes, olives and seasoning. Shave the Parmesan over the top and drizzle with olive oil and balsamic vinegar. Lightly mix and serve.

Greek salads are so much part of the easy, Mediterranean style of eating – a bit of crisp, a bit of fiery, a few baby herbs, some vinegary olives (and Greece produces some of the best) and salty anchovies. Use Kalamata olives, but unstoned, because they have more flavour. Warn anyone who will be eating the salad that the olives have stones.

1 iceberg lettuce, quartered and torn apart

about 250 g feta cheese, crumbled into big pieces, or cubed

about 200 g Kalamata olives

2 red onions, halved, then sliced into petals

2 mini–cucumbers, halved lengthways, then thinly sliced diagonally

4 big ripe red tomatoes, cut into chunks

8 anchovy fillets, or to taste

a few fresh oregano sprigs, torn

a few fresh mint sprigs, torn

GREEK DRESSING

6 tablespoons extra virgin olive oil, preferably Greek

2 tablespoons freshly squeezed lemon juice

sea salt and freshly ground black pepper

SERVES 4

big greek salad

Put the lettuce in a big bowl. Add the cheese, olives, onions, cucumbers and tomatoes.

To make the dressing, put the olive oil, lemon juice and some seasoning in a jug or bowl and beat with a fork, then pour onto the salad.

Top with the anchovies, oregano and mint, and serve.

1 kg cooked or tinned chickpeas, rinsed and drained

4 marinated artichoke hearts, well drained and halved

4 large sun-blushed tomatoes, (optional)

250 g very ripe cherry tomatoes, halved

8 spring onions, sliced diagonally

a handful of fresh basil, torn

a small handful of fresh chives, scissor-snipped

leaves from a small handful of fresh flat leaf parsley, chopped

50 g Parmesan

1 tablespoon black pepper, cracked with a mortar and pestle

DIJON DRESSING

6 tablespoons extra virgin olive oil

1 tablespoon freshly squeezed lemon juice or sherry vinegar

1 teaspoon Dijon mustard

1 small garlic clove, crushed

sea salt and freshly ground black pepper

SERVES 4

Chickpeas are the basis of some of the best lunchtime salads and vegetable accompaniments for main courses. Like all dried pulses, they drink up flavours, but unlike some, chickpeas can be relied upon not to fall apart. You can part-prepare them, so the dressing soaks into the chickpeas, then add the fresh ingredients just before serving. Sun-blushed tomatoes are available from Italian delis.

quick chickpea salad

To make the dressing, put the olive oil, lemon juice or vinegar, mustard and garlic in a bowl and beat with a fork. Season to taste. Add the chickpeas, artichoke hearts and sun-blushed tomatoes, if using, and toss in the dressing. Cover and chill for up to 4 hours.

When ready to serve, add the cherry tomatoes, spring onions, basil, chives and parsley. Stir gently, then shave the Parmesan over the top and sprinkle with the pepper.

Variations

• You can add any number of other ingredients, including olives, Parma ham, salami or chorizo, tinned or char-grilled fresh tuna, other vegetables, leaves or herbs, or your favourite spices.

• Instead of Dijon dressing, dress with basil oil or other herb oil. A few drops of chilli oil in the dressing instead of the mustard give a different kind of fire.

tuscan panzanella

6 very ripe, flavourful tomatoes

2 garlic cloves, sliced into slivers

4 thick slices of day-old bread, preferably Italian-style, such as pugliese or ciabatta

about 10 cm cucumber, halved, deseeded and finely sliced diagonally

1 red onion, chopped

1 tablespoon freshly chopped flat leaf parsley

8–12 tablespoons extra virgin olive oil

2 tablespoons white wine vinegar, cider vinegar or sherry vinegar

a handful of fresh basil, torn

12 caperberries or 4 tablespoons capers packed in brine, rinsed and drained

1 teaspoon balsamic vinegar (optional)

sea salt and freshly ground black pepper

SERVES 4

There are as many variations of this Tuscan bread salad as there are cooks – some old recipes don't even include tomatoes. The trick is to let the flavours blend well without allowing the bread to disintegrate into a mush. Always use the ripest, reddest, most flavourful tomatoes you can find – sweet Marmande, with its furrowed skin, is an ideal variety, or you could use one of the full-flavoured heirloom varieties, such as Black Russian or Green Zebra, or at least an Italian plum tomato.

Preheat the oven to 180°C (350°F) Gas 4.

Cut the tomatoes in half, spike with the slivers of garlic and roast in the preheated oven for about 1 hour, or until wilted and some of the moisture has evaporated.

Meanwhile, put the bread on an oiled stove-top grill pan and cook until lightly toasted and barred with grill marks on both sides. Tear or cut the toast into pieces and put into a salad bowl. Sprinkle with a little water until damp.

Add the tomatoes, cucumber, onion, parsley and some seasoning. Sprinkle with the olive oil and vinegar, toss well, then set aside for about 1 hour to develop the flavours.

Add the basil leaves, caperberries or capers and balsamic vinegar, if using, and serve.

1 egg, preferably free-range and organic

6 smallest leaves of cos lettuce (a young cos, not Little Gem)

½ tablespoon freshly squeezed lemon juice, plus 1 lemon cut into wedges, to serve (optional)

2 tablespoons extra virgin olive oil

3–4 tinned anchovy fillets, rinsed and drained

Parmesan shavings, at room temperature

sea salt and freshly ground black pepper

CROUTONS

1 thick slice of crusty white bread

2 tablespoons oil

1 garlic clove, crushed

SERVES 1

This is probably the most famous salad in the world and the perfect combination of salty, crispy crunch. It was invented by Italian chef Caesar Cardini in Tijuana, Mexico, in 1924. Note that this recipe serves one person but it's easily adapted to serve more.

caesar salad

To cook the egg, put it in a small saucepan and bring to the boil. Reduce the heat and simmer for 4–5 minutes. Remove from the heat and cover with cold water to stop it cooking further. Leave to cool a little, then peel. Cut into quarters just before serving.

To make the croutons, tear the bread into bite-sized chunks, brush with the oil and rub with the garlic. Cook on a preheated stove-top grill pan until crisply golden and barred with brown.

Put the lettuce into a large bowl add some seasoning and the lemon juice and toss with your hands. Finally, sprinkle with olive oil and toss again.

Put the croutons in a bowl and put the dressed leaves on top. Add the anchovies, egg and Parmesan, sprinkle with pepper and serve with lemon wedges, if using.

couscous with feta, dill and spring beans

275 g couscous

400 ml boiling water

5 tablespoons extra virgin olive oil

1 garlic clove, crushed

3 shallots, peeled and thinly sliced

2 tablespoons freshly chopped dill

2 tablespoons freshly chopped chives

1 tablespoon finely chopped preserved lemon, or 1 tablespoon zest and flesh of fresh unwaxed lemon, finely chopped

250 g feta cheese, chopped

150 g sugar snap peas

150 g frozen baby broad beans, defrosted

150 g frozen peas, defrosted

freshly ground black pepper

SERVES 4

Dill is a herb that has never been terribly fashionable, unlike its peers, rosemary and sage. It's quite a floral, grassy herb and a whiff of it conjures up springtime, which is possibly why it is so well complemented by the beans and peas in this dish. Marinating the feta lifts it from a salty, creamy cheese to something much more complex, so it's well worth it, even if it's just for 5 minutes.

Put the couscous in a large bowl and pour over the boiling water. Cover with clingfilm or a plate and leave to swell for 10 minutes.

Pour the olive oil into a mixing bowl and add the garlic, shallots, dill, chives and preserved or fresh lemon and lots of freshly ground black pepper – the coarser the better. Add the feta, turn in the oil and set aside while you cook the beans.

Bring a medium saucepan of unsalted water to the boil. Add the sugar snap peas, bring back to the boil and cook for 1 minute. Add the broad beans, bring back to the boil and cook for 1 minute. Finally, add the peas and cook for 2 minutes. Drain.

Uncover the couscous, stir in the hot beans, transfer to bowls and top with the feta, spooning over the flavoured oil as you go. Stir well before serving.

couscous salad with mint and coriander

4 tablespoons couscous

125 ml boiling chicken stock or water

6 sun-blushed tomatoes (see page 61) or 6 fresh cherry tomatoes, halved

2 marinated artichoke hearts, well drained and halved

3–4 spring onions, sliced

400 g tinned chickpeas, drained and rinsed

HARISSA DRESSING

6 tablespoons extra virgin olive oil

1 tablespoon sherry vinegar or cider vinegar

1 tablespoon harissa paste

sea salt and freshly ground black pepper

TO SERVE

a handful of fresh flat leaf parsley, coarsely chopped

watercress sprigs

fresh mint sprigs

fresh coriander sprigs

scissor-snipped fresh chives

SERVES 2

This very quick and easy salad is endlessly adaptable. Omit the chicken and add other uncooked or lightly blanched vegetables, such as cucumber, baby carrots, cherry tomatoes, sugar snap peas, asparagus tips or herbs. Easy-cook couscous is supposed to be just soaked then drained, but it's often better if it's microwaved or steamed after soaking. It should be dry and fluffy.

Put the couscous in a heatproof bowl and cover with the stock or water. Leave for 15 minutes until the water has been absorbed. For a fluffier texture, put the soaked couscous in a sieve and steam over simmering water for another 10 minutes, or microwave in the bowl on 50 per cent for about 5 minutes. Drain if necessary, pressing the liquid through the sieve with a spoon, then fluff up with a fork. Leave to cool.

Put the couscous in a bowl, add the tomatoes, artichoke hearts, spring onions and chickpeas. Keep the watercress and herbs in a separate container until just before serving.

To make the dressing, put the olive oil, vinegar and harissa paste in a bowl and beat with a fork. Season to taste. Sprinkle half the dressing over the couscous mixture and toss with a fork. Add the watercress and herbs and serve. Serve the extra dressing separately.

Variation This is a perfect picnic, lunchbox or make-ahead salad. Put the watercress and herbs into a small container and seal. Put the dressing ingredients in a screw-top jar, and shake to mix. Shake again just before serving. Put the couscous and remaining ingredients in a lidded plastic bowl, and seal until ready to use. To serve, add the dressing, parsley and watercress and toss well.

chicken, apple and peanut salad

2 apples, cored and chopped

1 tablespoon freshly squeezed lemon juice

100 g baby spinach leaves, lightly rinsed

300 g grilled chicken breast, chopped

1 tablespoon unsalted roasted peanuts

4 tomatoes, chopped

½ small cucumber, chopped

2 tablespoons balsamic vinegar

sea salt and freshly ground black pepper

1 lemon, cut into wedges, to serve (optional)

SERVES 4

Peanuts are nutritional powerhouses. Not only do they provide you with eight vitamins and 13 minerals – including some that are hard to find naturally, such as magnesium and zinc – they contain plant chemicals which can help to protect against cancer. So this is an incredibly health-giving lunchtime salad!

Put the apples in a bowl, sprinkle with the lemon juice and toss to coat. Add the spinach, chicken, peanuts, tomatoes and cucumber.

Pour the balsamic vinegar over the salad, season and toss well. Serve with lemon wedges, if using.

Variation This salad also tastes great with flaked smoked mackerel fillets instead of the chicken.

60 g small pasta shapes

2 tablespoons stoned black or green olives or 2 tablespoons cooked sweetcorn

5 cm cucumber, roughly chopped

5 cherry tomatoes, halved

200 g tinned tuna, drained and flaked

a few fresh chives, scissor-snipped

OLIVE OIL DRESSING

2 tablespoons olive oil

1 tablespoon freshly squeezed lemon juice

½ teaspoon Dijon or mild mustard

a pinch of salt

a pinch of freshly ground black pepper

SERVES 2

Small shell or 'bow-tie' pasta works best here. The dressing is a tangy lemon and olive oil, and you could use cooked sweetcorn instead of the olives.

tuna pasta salad

Cook the pasta in salted boiling water according to the manufacturer's instructions.

Drain the pasta in a colander and rinse it under cold water so it cools quickly and rinses off the starch. Leave to drain thoroughly in the colander while you make the rest of the salad.

Put the olives, cucumber, tomatoes, tuna and chives in a bowl.

Put all the ingredients for the dressing in a screw-top jar and shake well. Season to taste.

Pour the dressing over the salad, then mix everything very gently with a metal spoon. Cover tightly and store in the refrigerator for up to 48 hours.

Most people love noodles, and the delicate spiciness in this recipe should not overpower sensitive taste buds. However, you can deseed the chillies if you prefer a milder flavour. Make this quick, tasty recipe for a weekday dinner, then take the leftovers into work for a satisfying lunch the next day.

thai chicken noodle salad

1 tablespoon vegetable oil

350 g chicken breast, thinly sliced

1 cm fresh ginger,
peeled and chopped

2 garlic cloves, crushed

1 lemongrass stalk, thinly sliced

1 medium-hot red or green chilli,
finely diced

300 g thick noodles

100 g pak-choi, chopped

4 lime wedges, to serve

SERVES 4

Heat the vegetable oil in a wok or large frying pan, add the chicken, ginger, garlic, lemongrass and chilli and stir well. Cook over medium heat for 5 minutes, or until the chicken is cooked through and the lemongrass has softened.

Meanwhile, cook the noodles according to the manufacturer's instructions, then drain.

Add the pak-choi and cooked noodles to the wok and toss well. Serve with wedges of lime.

turkey cobb salad

4 streaky bacon rashers

2 Hass avocados

1 large butterhead lettuce

6 ripe plum tomatoes, cut into wedges

500 g cooked turkey, shredded, at room temperature

2 hard-boiled eggs, quartered

100 g Roquefort cheese, cut into thin slices, or crumbled

olive oil, for cooking

LEMON CREAM DRESSING

250 ml double cream

freshly squeezed juice of 1 lemon

a handful of fresh chives, scissor-snipped

TO SERVE

crusty rolls

mini-cornichons, halved lengthways, or sliced gherkins

SERVES 4

This American classic was invented in the Roaring Twenties by a Californian restaurateur named Cobb. It's essentially a 'bitser' salad – bitser this and bitser that – just like Niçoise or Gado Gado, two other legendary mixed salads. It's also a good post-turkey dish, when you have lots of turkey left over and you're looking for an effortless way to serve it. Traditionally, the ingredients were arranged in lines but this version is jumbled together. The dressing is a lighter, fresher take on the customary mayonnaise.

Brush a frying pan with olive oil, add the bacon and cook until crispy but not crumbly. Remove and drain on crumpled kitchen paper.

Cut the avocados in half, remove the stones, then scoop out the flesh with a teaspoon.

Share the bacon, lettuce, tomatoes, turkey, eggs, cheese and avocado between 4 plates or bowls.

To make the dressing, put the cream in a bowl, add the lemon juice and beat well. Stir in the chives, then spoon over the salad and serve with crusty rolls and cornichons.

MAIN COURSES

tagine of butternut squash, shallots, sultanas and almonds

3 tablespoons olive oil with a knob of butter

about 12 pink shallots, peeled and left whole

about 8 garlic cloves, lightly crushed

120 g sultanas

120 g blanched almonds

1–2 teaspoons harissa paste

2 tablespoons dark, runny honey

1 medium butternut squash, halved lengthways, peeled, deseeded and sliced

sea salt and freshly ground black pepper

a small handful of fresh coriander, finely chopped, to serve

1 lemon, cut into wedges, to serve

SERVES 3–4

Substantial enough for a main meal, served with couscous and yoghurt, vegetable tagines also make good side dishes for grilled or roasted meats or other tagines. You can cook this one in the oven if you like, using a tagine base or an ovenproof pan.

Heat the oil and butter in a tagine or heavy-based casserole. Stir in the shallots and garlic and sauté them until they begin to colour. Add the sultanas and almonds and stir in the harissa paste and honey. Toss in the squash, making sure it is coated in the spicy oil. Pour in enough water to cover the base of the tagine and cover with the lid. Cook gently for 15–20 minutes, until the shallots and squash are tender but still quite firm.

Season to taste, sprinkle the coriander leaves over the top and serve with wedges of lemon to squeeze over the dish.

For nights when you want dinner in a hurry, this can be on the table in just 10 minutes. Serve with couscous or a mixture of basmati and wild rice, together with some green beans or cabbage.

½ small onion, sliced

150 ml vegetable stock

150 g mixed mushrooms, chopped if large

1 garlic clove, crushed

1 teaspoon wholegrain mustard

½ teaspoon tomato purée

1 tablespoon crème fraîche

sea salt and freshly ground black pepper

TO SERVE

freshly chopped parsley

couscous or a mixture of basmati and wild rice

green beans or cabbage

SERVES 1

mustardy mushroom stroganoff

Cook the onion in a covered saucepan with 3 tablespoons of the stock for about 4 minutes or until softened and the liquid has evaporated.

Stir in the mushrooms, garlic and seasoning, then add the remaining stock, mustard and tomato purée.

Cook, covered, for 2 minutes, then remove the lid and cook rapidly for 2 minutes to reduce the liquid to a syrup. Stir in the crème fraîche and parsley and serve immediately on a bed of couscous or rice, with green beans or cabbage on the side.

calabrian-style potatoes and peppers

150 ml olive oil

1 red pepper, halved, deseeded and thickly sliced

1 yellow pepper, halved, deseeded and thickly sliced

550 g potatoes, thinly sliced

sea salt and freshly ground black pepper

SERVES 4

This is a fine example of the 'less is more' approach to cooking – simple, good-quality ingredients cooked to perfection.

Heat the olive oil in a large, lidded frying pan. Add the red and yellow peppers and cook for 10 minutes, stirring occasionally, until starting to turn golden brown. Add the potatoes and some seasoning to the pan, cover with a lid and cook for 5 minutes.

Remove the lid and continue cooking for 15 minutes, turning every few minutes as the potatoes begin to brown, taking care not to break them. If the potatoes start to stick, this will just add to the flavour of the dish, but don't let them burn.

When the potatoes are tender, transfer to a serving dish and leave to cool for 5 minutes before serving.

rice and bean burgers

200 g brown rice
(not quick-cook variety)

2 tablespoons
Worcestershire sauce

1 onion, chopped

2 garlic cloves, crushed

200 g tinned cannellini beans,
drained and rinsed

200 g tinned red kidney beans,
drained and rinsed

50 g fresh wholemeal breadcrumbs

1 egg, beaten

115 g mature Cheddar, grated

2 tablespoons freshly
chopped thyme

1 small green pepper,
deseeded and chopped

1 large carrot, coarsely grated

wholemeal flour or cornmeal,
for coating

2–3 tablespoons sunflower oil

sea salt and freshly ground
black pepper

TO SERVE

salad leaves

relish

MAKES 10–12

There's something really satisfying about making your own burgers. These need to chill for 1½ hours so start them in advance. Pop any leftover burgers in the freezer before you cook them and take them out as and when you need them.

Cook the rice according to the manufacturer's instructions, leaving it to overcook slightly so that it is soft. Drain the rice, transfer it to a large bowl and reserve. Put 2 tablespoons water and the Worcestershire sauce in a frying pan, add the onion and garlic and cook over medium heat until softened, about 8 minutes.

Put the onion, garlic, cooked rice, beans, breadcrumbs, egg, cheese and thyme in a food processor. Add plenty of seasoning, then process until combined. Add the green pepper and grated carrot and mix well. Refrigerate for 1½ hours, or until quite firm.

Shape the mixture into 10–12 burgers, using wet hands if the mixture sticks. Coat them in flour or cornmeal and chill for a further 30 minutes. Preheat the oven to 190°C (375°F) Gas 5.

Put the burgers on a non-stick baking sheet and brush lightly with a little oil. Cook in the preheated oven for 20–25 minutes, or until piping hot. Alternatively, heat the oil in a non-stick frying pan and fry the burgers for 3–4 minutes on each side, or until piping hot. Serve immediately with salad leaves and relish.

Variation Add 1–2 deseeded finely chopped chillies to give an extra bite and 3 finely chopped celery sticks to add some crunch.

polenta pizza tart

sea salt and freshly ground
black pepper

leafy salad, to serve

PIZZA BASE

400 ml vegetable stock

75 g powdered polenta
or cornmeal

15 g Parmesan, freshly grated

PIZZA TOPPING

400 g tinned chopped tomatoes

1 garlic clove, crushed

2 tablespoons freshly chopped basil

1 small courgette, thinly sliced

½ red and ½ yellow pepper,
deseeded and thinly sliced

50 g mushrooms, sliced

½ small red onion, thinly sliced

1 teaspoon olive oil

60 g mozzarella cheese, sliced

10 g Parmesan, freshly grated

*a tart tin, 23 cm in diameter,
lightly greased*

SERVES 4

This has all the flavour of a pizza, but with a polenta base instead of pizza dough. It makes the perfect no-fuss family dinner, which everyone will love.

Preheat the oven to 200°C (400°F) Gas 6.

Bring the stock to the boil in a large saucepan. Pour in the polenta in a steady stream and stir until bubbling. Reduce the heat and cook for 5 minutes, stirring occasionally, until thickened. Take care to protect your hand, as the bubbling polenta tends to spit. Remove from the heat and stir in the Parmesan and seasoning. Pour into the prepared tart tin and leave to cool and firm up for 10–15 minutes.

Tip the chopped tomatoes into a saucepan, add the garlic, basil and seasoning and simmer briskly for 10 minutes until thickened. Spread over the polenta base.

Mix the courgette, peppers, mushrooms and onion with the olive oil to coat, season lightly and pile on top of the base. Bake in the preheated oven for 10 minutes, then scatter the cheeses over the pizza tart. Return to the oven for 5 minutes, until the mozzarella starts to melt.

Cut into wedges and serve with a leafy salad.

3 tablespoons peanut or
sunflower oil

1 onion, sliced

2 garlic cloves, chopped

3 cm fresh ginger,
peeled and grated

1 tablespoon hot curry paste

1 teaspoon ground cinnamon

500 g potatoes, cubed

400 g tinned chopped tomatoes

300 ml vegetable stock

1 tablespoon tomato purée

200 g button mushrooms, halved

200 g frozen peas

25 g ground almonds

2 tablespoons freshly
chopped coriander

sea salt and freshly ground
black pepper

basmati rice, to serve

SERVES 4

quick vegetable curry

This is a super-easy, quick and tasty cheat's curry
because it is made with ready-made curry paste.
Serve with basmati rice.

Heat the oil in a saucepan and fry the onion, garlic, ginger, curry
paste and cinnamon for 5 minutes. Add the potatoes, tomatoes,
stock, tomato purée and some seasoning. Bring to the boil, cover
and simmer gently for 20 minutes.

Add the mushrooms, peas, ground almonds and coriander to the pan
and cook for a further 10 minutes. Taste and adjust the seasoning if
necessary. Serve with basmati rice.

Courgettes are so flavourful when cooked this way – bathed in garlic and olive oil, then stuffed with sweet, ripe cherry tomatoes and enveloped in melting fontina cheese. A delightfully fresh and summery supper.

6 medium courgettes

2 garlic cloves, chopped

2 tablespoons olive oil, plus extra for sprinkling

about 30 cherry tomatoes, halved

3–4 tablespoons dried breadcrumbs

250 g fontina cheese, sliced

sea salt and freshly ground black pepper

a shallow ovenproof dish, greased

SERVES 6

courgettes and tomatoes
baked with fontina

Preheat the oven to 160°C (325°F) Gas 3.

Halve the courgettes lengthways and trim a little off the uncut sides so that they will sit still like boats. Using a teaspoon, scoop out the soft-seeded centres. Arrange the boats in a row in the prepared dish.

Put the garlic, olive oil and some seasoning in a bowl, stir well, then brush over the cut surfaces of the courgettes. Arrange the halved tomatoes in the grooves. Season well, then sprinkle with olive oil and breadcrumbs. Bake in the preheated oven for 30 minutes.

Remove from the oven and arrange the cheese over the courgettes and tomatoes. Return the dish to the oven for another 10 minutes to melt the cheese. Serve immediately while the cheese is still bubbling.

oven-roasted vegetables
with rosemary, bay leaves and garlic

500 g ratte or other salad
potatoes, cut into 5-cm chunks

about 500 g butternut squash,
cut into wedges and deseeded

6 small red onions, quartered

4 tablespoons extra virgin olive oil

8 garlic cloves (unpeeled)

2 red romano (long) peppers,
deseeded and cut into chunks

4 fresh rosemary sprigs

4 fresh bay leaf sprigs

sea salt

a large roasting tin

SERVES 4

Roasted vegetables are made extra special with the strong flavours of herbs. Thyme is good, but rosemary is even better (be sparing though – too much can overwhelm a dish). Bay leaves are quite mild when young, so don't use as many if you have mature leaves.

Preheat the oven to 200°C (400°F) Gas 6.

Bring a large saucepan of water to the boil, add salt and the potatoes and cook for 5 minutes. Drain, then put in the roasting tin. Add the squash, onions and 2 tablespoons of the oil. Toss to coat, then roast in the preheated oven for 10 minutes.

Add 1 extra tablespoon of oil to the roasting tin, followed by the garlic and peppers, 2 of the rosemary sprigs and 2 of the bay sprigs. Roast for 15 minutes, then add the rest of the herbs and continue roasting for 10–15 minutes. Turn the vegetables occasionally until they are all tender and the edges slightly charred. Trail the remaining oil over the top.

Variation Sprinkle with 3 tablespoons pine nuts and some crumbled feta cheese 5 minutes before the end of the cooking time, so the nuts roast a little and the feta softens.

Fresh or frozen spinach can be used in this recipe, but do make sure that both are thoroughly drained.

macaroni, spinach and cheese bake

250 g macaroni

50 g butter

50 g plain flour

500 ml milk

150 g cooked spinach, well drained

200 g Parmesan, freshly grated

sea salt and freshly ground black pepper

a large ovenproof dish

SERVES 4

Cook the macaroni according to the manufacturer's instructions. Preheat the oven to 190°C (375°F) Gas 5.

Meanwhile, melt the butter in a saucepan, remove from the heat and mix in the flour to make a *roux*. Return to a low heat and slowly pour in the milk, stirring constantly. Bring to the boil and cook for 1 minute, stirring frequently.

Drain the macaroni and add to the sauce along with the spinach, seasoning and half the cheese. Mix well. Pour the mixture into the ovenproof dish, scatter the remaining cheese on top and bake in the preheated oven for 15 minutes, until golden.

A simple and stylish pasta dish to cook at home, this traditional Italian recipe never seems to lose its appeal. Anchovies, either in oil or salted, are very good, as are tiny, compact capers. Buy them from a good Italian deli if you can. Both these ingredients are real gems that help make this piquant storecupboard dish just as memorable as it can be when eaten on holiday.

300 g spaghetti

4 tomatoes, skinned (see page 19), deseeded and chopped

150 g stoned black olives

75 g tinned anchovies, chopped

3 tablespoons capers

leaves from a large handful of fresh flat leaf parsley, chopped

4 tablespoons olive oil

freshly ground black pepper

75 g Parmesan, freshly grated, to serve

SERVES 4

spaghetti puttanesca

Bring a large saucepan of water to the boil. Add the spaghetti, stir well to separate the strands and simmer for 9 minutes.

When the spaghetti is cooked, drain it thoroughly. Dry the saucepan, then return the spaghetti to the pan and add the tomatoes, olives, anchovies, capers, parsley and olive oil. Season with pepper.

Toss the pasta well and serve with a dish of freshly grated Parmesan for sprinkling.

cannelloni with ricotta, bitter greens and cherry tomato sauce

12 dried cannelloni tubes or
12 sheets fresh or dried lasagne

TOMATO SAUCE

3 tablespoons olive oil

2 garlic cloves, finely chopped

750 g cherry tomatoes, halved

3 tablespoons freshly chopped basil

sea salt and freshly ground
black pepper

RICOTTA FILLING

100 g bitter salad greens, such as
rocket, watercress or spinach

500 g ricotta cheese

2 eggs, beaten

100 g Parmesan, freshly grated

freshly grated nutmeg, to taste

a piping bag with a large plain nozzle

a shallow ovenproof dish, greased

SERVES 4–6

This version of cannelloni combines a creamy sharp ricotta filling speckled with slightly bitter greens and a sweet tomato sauce. The contrast between the sauce and filling is amazing. The greens used here are easily available – rocket, watercress or spinach.

Preheat the oven to 200°C (400°F) Gas 6.

To make the tomato sauce, heat the oil in a saucepan, add the garlic and cook until just turning golden. Add the halved tomatoes. They should hiss as they go in – this will slightly caramelize the juices, and concentrate the flavour. Stir well, then simmer for 10 minutes. Stir in the basil and season (the sauce should still be quite lumpy). Set aside.

To make the ricotta filling, plunge the salad greens into a saucepan of boiling water for 1 minute, then drain well, squeezing out any excess moisture. Chop finely. Press the ricotta through a sieve into a bowl. Beat in the eggs, then add the chopped greens and half the Parmesan. Season with nutmeg, salt and pepper. Set aside.

Cook the cannelloni or lasagne sheets in a large saucepan of salted boiling water according to the manufacturer's instructions. Lift out of the water and drain on a clean tea towel.

Spoon the ricotta filling into the piping bag. Fill each tube of cannelloni or pipe down the shorter edge of each lasagne sheet and roll it up. Arrange the filled cannelloni tightly together in a single layer in the prepared dish. Spoon over the tomato sauce and sprinkle with the remaining Parmesan. Bake in the preheated oven for 25–30 minutes until bubbling. Serve immediately.

pasta with fresh tomato

1 kg ripe tomatoes

6 tablespoons extra virgin
olive oil

2 red chillies,
deseeded and chopped

2 garlic cloves, crushed

a bunch of fresh basil, chopped

1 teaspoon caster sugar

350 g spaghetti

cracked black pepper

freshly grated Pecorino Sardo or
Parmesan, to serve

SERVES 4

This sauce is best made as soon as the new season's tomatoes arrive in the shops, especially the vine-ripened varieties that we see more and more. Use the instructions on page 19 for an easy way to skin the tomatoes.

Skin the tomatoes according to the instructions on page 19, then put into a bowl. Add the oil, chillies, garlic, basil, sugar and seasoning and leave to infuse while you cook the pasta (or longer if possible).

Cook the pasta according to the manufacturer's instructions. Drain well and immediately stir in the fresh tomato sauce. Serve at once with the grated Parmesan.

This is a great mid-week supper dish and just as good if people are coming over. It's also nice to have a change from tomato-based sauces. Pancetta is easy to find in supermarkets now so do use that rather than bacon – pancetta is not as smoky and strong and its subtlety is just what's needed here.

linguine with peas, pancetta and sage

300 g peas, fresh or frozen and defrosted

3–5 tablespoons extra virgin olive oil

5 tablespoons fresh breadcrumbs

500 g linguine

90 g thinly sliced pancetta, chopped

3 garlic cloves, crushed

a few fresh sage sprigs, leaves finely chopped

5 tablespoons dry white wine

25 g Parmesan, freshly grated

a small handful of fresh flat leaf parsley, chopped

fine sea salt and freshly ground black pepper

SERVES 4–6

Lightly blanch the peas in a pan of boiling water for 2–3 minutes. Drain and set aside.

Heat 2 tablespoons of the oil in a frying pan. Add the breadcrumbs and cook until toasted, stirring occasionally, about 3 minutes. Season lightly and set aside.

Cook the pasta in a large saucepan of salted boiling water according to the manufacturer's instructions.

Heat the remaining oil in a saucepan large enough to hold all the pasta later. Add the pancetta and cook, stirring, until browned, about 2 minutes. Add the garlic and cook, stirring for 1 minute; don't let the garlic burn. Stir in the sage and wine. Cook, stirring until the liquid has almost evaporated, about 1 minute. Set aside until needed.

Drain the cooked pasta thoroughly and add to the pan of pancetta. Add the peas and 1–2 tablespoons more oil and cook over low heat, tossing well to mix. Stir in the cheese, parsley and pepper; taste and add more seasoning if necessary. Sprinkle with the breadcrumbs.

In Italy, pork is often braised with milk, as it tenderizes the meat and the juices mingle with the milk to provide a sweet, meaty sauce. Rosemary is lovely with pork but you could use chopped sage – just add it earlier when you brown the pork.

rigatoni with pork and lemon ragu

2 tablespoons olive oil

400 g minced pork

1 onion, finely chopped

2 garlic cloves, thinly sliced

4 anchovy fillets in oil, drained

2 tablespoons fresh rosemary leaves

finely grated zest and freshly squeezed juice of 1 unwaxed lemon

375 g rigatoni

500 ml whole milk

75 g green olives, stoned and chopped

75 ml double cream

a good grating of fresh nutmeg

4 tablespoons Parmesan shavings, plus extra to serve

sea salt and freshly ground black pepper

SERVES 4

Put a large saucepan of salted water on to boil for the rigatoni.

Meanwhile, heat the olive oil in a large frying pan over high heat and add the pork. Leave it for a few minutes until it browns, then turn it over and allow the other side to brown too. Add the onion, garlic, anchovies, rosemary and lemon zest and stir to combine with the pork. Reduce the heat, cover and leave the onion to soften for 10 minutes, stirring occasionally so the ingredients don't stick to the bottom of the pan.

When the salted water in the large pan is boiling, add the rigatoni and cook according to the manufacturer's instructions until al dente.

When the onion is translucent, add the milk, lemon juice and olives, and bring to the boil, uncovered, scraping the base of the pan to loosen any sticky, flavoursome bits and incorporating them into the sauce. Simmer for about 15–20 minutes, or until about two-thirds of the liquid has evaporated and the pork is soft. Stir in the cream, then season with salt, pepper and nutmeg.

Drain the rigatoni, put it back into its pan and spoon in the pork ragu. Add the Parmesan shavings, stir well and transfer to bowls. Sprinkle the extra Parmesan shavings on top.

This uncomplicated pomodoro sauce relies upon using the best tinned Italian peeled plum tomatoes you can find. The milk-soaked bread and Parmesan keep the meatballs feather-light and impossibly moreish.

spaghetti and meatballs

400 g minced pork or beef

1 small onion, very finely chopped

1 egg, beaten

5 garlic cloves, finely chopped

3 tablespoons freshly chopped flat leaf parsley

3 tablespoons freshly grated Parmesan, plus extra to serve

1 teaspoon each salt and freshly ground pepper

2 slices of white bread

3 tablespoons milk

5 tablespoons olive oil

three 400-g tins whole, peeled plum tomatoes

1 tablespoon butter

400 g spaghetti

SERVES 4

Preheat the oven to 200°C (400°F) Gas 6.

Combine the pork, onion, egg, most of the garlic, parsley, Parmesan and some seasoning. Put the bread in a separate bowl and pour over the milk. Break the mixture up into small pieces then add to the bowl with the meat. Mix everything with your hands until well combined. Roll into 5-cm balls and place on a baking sheet lined with greaseproof paper or aluminium foil. Bake in the preheated oven for 15 minutes, giving the meatballs a shake halfway through cooking so they don't stick. Set aside.

In a large, wide saucepan, heat the olive oil and cook the remaining garlic until golden but not brown. Add the tomatoes and break up with a flat spoon. Season. Cook over medium/high heat for 15 minutes, stirring every 5 minutes or so. Keep a splatter screen on while cooking. The sauce should be thick when it is done. Add the butter and the meatballs.

Boil the spaghetti in plenty of salted water until it is just al dente. Drain and mix with the sauce. Serve sprinkled with grated Parmesan.

This is a great way to use up leftover spaghetti. The spaghetti is mixed with fresh arrabbiata sauce made with tomatoes and chillies to add a fiery kick.

spaghetti and rocket frittata

3 tablespoons extra virgin olive oil

1 onion, chopped

1 garlic clove, crushed

3 ripe plum tomatoes, chopped

1 fresh red chilli, deseeded and finely chopped

2 tablespoons tomato purée

150 ml white wine or water

325 g cold cooked spaghetti (140 g before cooking)

6 large eggs

2 tablespoons freshly grated Parmesan

25 g rocket

2 tablespoons balsamic vinegar

sea salt and freshly ground black pepper

a 24-cm heavy non-stick frying pan (measure the base, not the top)

SERVES 4

Heat 1 tablespoon of the oil in a saucepan, add the onion and sauté for 5 minutes until softened. Add the garlic, tomatoes and chilli and cook for 3–4 minutes, stirring several times. Add the tomato purée and wine or water and simmer for 5 minutes. Remove from the heat, add the spaghetti and toss gently.

Break the eggs into a large bowl and whisk briefly with a fork. Add the spaghetti and sauce and mix gently.

Heat the remaining oil in the frying pan, add the spaghetti and egg mixture and cook over low heat for 10–12 minutes, or until golden brown on the underside and almost set on the top. Meanwhile, preheat the grill.

Sprinkle with the Parmesan and slide under the preheated grill for 30–60 seconds to melt the cheese and finish cooking the top. Leave to cool for 5 minutes, then transfer to a plate. Put the rocket on top of the frittata, sprinkle with balsamic vinegar and serve.

There's something uniquely comforting about risotto. It's like nursery food for adults. And when it's made with autumnal squash and woody sage, it becomes the perfect one-bowl meal to serve up on a cold, dark evening in front of the television. It tastes wonderful on its own or served with grilled lamb chops.

butternut squash, sage and chilli risotto

about 1.5 litres hot chicken or vegetable stock

125 g unsalted butter

1 large onion, finely chopped

1–2 fresh or dried red chillies, deseeded and finely chopped

500 g fresh butternut squash or pumpkin, peeled, deseeded and finely diced

500 g risotto rice

3 tablespoons freshly chopped sage

75 g Parmesan, freshly grated

sea salt and freshly ground black pepper

SERVES 6

Pour the stock into a saucepan and keep at a gentle simmer. Melt half the butter in a large, heavy saucepan and add the onion. Cook gently for 10 minutes until soft, golden and translucent but not browned. Stir in the chopped chillies and cook for 1 minute. Add the butternut or pumpkin and cook, stirring constantly, for 5 minutes, until it begins to soften slightly. Stir in the rice to coat with the butter and vegetables. Cook for a few minutes to toast the grains.

Begin adding the stock, a large ladle at a time, stirring gently until each ladle has almost been absorbed by the rice. The risotto should be barely simmering throughout cooking, so don't let the rice dry out – add more stock as necessary. Continue until the rice is tender and creamy, but the grains still firm and the squash beginning to disintegrate. (This should take 15–20 minutes depending on the type of rice used – check the manufacturer's instructions.)

Season to taste and stir in the sage, remaining butter and all the Parmesan. Cover, leave to rest for a couple of minutes, then serve.

Ideal for an indulgent lunch or supper dish, this creamy rice cake oozes with mozzarella, and has pockets of tomatoes that burst with flavour. You could even add a layer of cubed mozzarella to the middle of the tart, so that the centre exudes strings of melted cheese when you cut it.

30 g powdered polenta or dried breadcrumbs

500 g fresh or 250 g frozen whole leaf spinach, thawed

3 eggs, beaten

250 g risotto rice (not long-grain)

1 tablespoon olive oil

25 g butter

1 onion, finely chopped

freshly grated nutmeg

150 g tiny cherry tomatoes

175 g mozzarella cheese, cubed

4 tablespoons freshly grated Parmesan

sea salt and freshly ground black pepper

a 20-cm non-stick springform cake tin, heavily greased

SERVES 6

three-coloured rice and cheese cake

Preheat the oven to 200°C (400°F) Gas 6. Dust the prepared cake tin with the polenta or dried breadcrumbs.

If using fresh spinach, tear off the stems. Wash the leaves well, then put them, still wet, in a covered saucepan and cook for a few minutes until wilted. Drain well but do not squeeze dry – you want large pieces of spinach. If using thawed spinach, lightly squeeze it to remove excess moisture and toss the leaves a little to loosen them. Mix the spinach into the beaten eggs.

Cook the rice in a large saucepan of salted boiling water for about 10 minutes, until almost tender, then drain. Heat the oil and butter in a frying pan. Add the onion and cook until golden. Stir into the rice.

Season the egg and spinach mixture with nutmeg, salt and pepper. Stir into the rice, then fold in the cherry tomatoes, cubed mozzarella and Parmesan. Spoon into the prepared cake tin and level the surface.

Bake in the preheated oven for 25–30 minutes, until firm and golden. Turn out and serve hot, cut into wedges.

chicken and barley supper

Healthy, wholesome and satisfying, this is the kind of meal that needs plenty of time on the stove to become really tasty and tender. In the meantime, you can put your feet up and relax.

2 tablespoons wholemeal flour

500 g skinless, boneless chicken breasts, cubed

100 g lean bacon rashers, cut into strips

2 medium onions, chopped

2 carrots, sliced

2 celery sticks, chopped

750–900 ml white wine or chicken stock

3 tablespoons pearl barley, rinsed

1 tablespoon freshly chopped mixed herbs, such as rosemary, basil, parsley and thyme, plus extra to serve

freshly ground black pepper

SERVES 4

Season the flour with black pepper, then toss the chicken cubes in the flour. Heat a large non-stick frying pan or saucepan, add the bacon and dry-fry for 5 minutes, stirring frequently, until the fat starts to run. Add the chicken and sauté for 5–8 minutes, turning frequently, until the chicken is sealed all over. Remove the chicken and bacon from the pan with a slotted spoon and set aside.

Add the onion, carrots, celery and 4 tablespoons of the wine or stock to the pan and sauté for 5 minutes, until the vegetables are softened. Add the pearl barley, herbs and 600 ml of the wine or stock. Bring to the boil, then cover, reduce the heat and simmer for 1 hour. Add more wine or stock as it is absorbed.

Return the chicken and bacon to the pan and continue to simmer for a further 30 minutes, or until the pearl barley and chicken are tender. Stir occasionally during cooking, adding a little more wine or stock, if necessary. Serve sprinkled with more chopped herbs and accompanied by a selection of your favourite vegetables.

Variation Use half the amount of chicken and cook as above. Once all the ingredients are tender, use a slotted spoon to remove 2–3 tablespoons of the mixture and reserve. Put the remainder in a food processor and blend to form a purée. Return to a clean saucepan together with the reserved ingredients. Heat until piping hot, adding a little extra stock or water to make a warming winter soup. You could do the same with any leftovers, taking care when reheating to make sure that it is piping hot.

There is a wonderful fragrance to Thai curries, and they make a fantastic family meal. Build up the chilli content gradually until you find a spiciness that everyone enjoys. Plain jasmine rice is a good accompaniment.

2 tablespoons vegetable oil

1 onion, sliced

5 cm fresh ginger, peeled and sliced

2 garlic cloves, crushed

1 lemongrass stalk, chopped

1 mild green chilli, diced

4 chicken fillets, sliced

2 kaffir lime leaves

2 tablespoons Thai green curry paste

200 ml coconut milk

freshly squeezed juice of 1 lime

75 g broccoli florets

75 g green beans, trimmed

sea salt and freshly ground black pepper

jasmine rice, to serve

SERVES 4

thai green curry

Heat the oil in a large saucepan, add the onion, ginger, garlic, lemongrass and chilli and cook over low heat for 5 minutes. Add the chicken and cook for a further 5 minutes.

Add the kaffir lime leaves and curry paste and mix well. Shake the tin of coconut milk and slowly pour into the curry, mixing constantly. Pour in 100 ml water and the lime juice, bring to a simmer and cook gently for 5 minutes. Add the broccoli and beans and simmer for another 3 minutes. Serve with boiled jasmine rice.

chicken and bacon pot

1 tablespoon olive oil

300 g bacon lardons

250 g button mushrooms

4 chicken breasts

1 garlic clove, crushed

2 shallots, diced

50 g plain flour

500 ml chicken stock

200 ml white wine

1 bay leaf

a handful of fresh parsley, chopped

sea salt and freshly ground black pepper

a mixture of basmati and wild rice, to serve

SERVES 4

The bacon lardons add a special intensity to the flavour of this easy-to-make dish. Serve with rice to mop up the lovely sauce.

Preheat the oven to 180°C (350°F) Gas 4.

Heat the olive oil in a casserole dish, add the lardons and mushrooms and cook over medium heat until golden. Transfer to a plate.

Put the chicken breasts in the casserole and quickly brown on both sides. Set aside with the lardons.

Sauté the garlic and shallots over low heat in the same pan for 5 minutes. Add the flour and mix well. Remove the pan from the heat, slowly pour in the stock and wine, and stir until smooth. Return to the heat and bring to the boil, stirring constantly. Mix in the lardons and mushrooms, then add the chicken breasts, bay leaf and seasoning. Cover and cook in the oven for 30 minutes. Add the parsley just before serving with rice.

This is a popular cold salad and a tasty way to use up leftover roast chicken. The creamy peanut butter dressing sets it apart from other salads.

bang bang chicken

400 g cooked boneless chicken, such as smoked chicken, cold roast chicken or cold turkey

1 large carrot

salad leaves, such as crispy lettuce or Chinese leaves, about 75 g

1 medium cucumber, cut into strips

BANG BANG DRESSING

5 tablespoons crunchy peanut butter

1 spring onion, very thinly sliced

1 teaspoon sesame oil

1 teaspoon soy sauce

1 teaspoon caster sugar

1 teaspoon Chinese white rice vinegar or cider vinegar

1 teaspoon rice wine or water

3 tablespoons hot water

SERVES 4

Remove any skin from the chicken and discard. Pull or cut the chicken into shreds. Shred the carrot with a vegetable peeler to make ultra-thin long ribbons.

Tear any large salad leaves into bite-sized pieces. Arrange the leaves on a serving dish. Scatter the cucumber sticks and carrot ribbons over the leaves. Arrange the chicken on the top.

To make the dressing, put the peanut butter, spring onion, sesame oil, soy sauce, sugar, vinegar, rice wine or water and hot water to the bowl. Stir gently until well mixed. Taste the dressing – it should be a harmonious balance of salty, sweet and sour flavours, so add more vinegar, sugar or soy as you think is needed. The dressing should be just thin enough to spoon over the chicken, so if it is too thick stir in another tablespoon or so of hot water.

When the sauce seems perfect, spoon it over the chicken and serve.

Mildly spicy and full of flavour, these chicken balls are made with your hands, then simply baked in the oven – no frying needed. Serve with Thai fragrant rice and extra sweet chilli sauce for dipping. Super easy and super delicious.

thai meatballs with chicken

50 g fresh breadcrumbs

500 g minced chicken or turkey

1 egg

2 spring onions, very thinly sliced

½ teaspoon ground coriander

a small handful of fresh coriander
leaves, about 15 g, chopped

1 teaspoon fish sauce or soy sauce

2 teaspoons sweet chilli sauce,
plus extra for serving

Thai fragrant rice, to serve

a large baking dish, oiled

MAKES 12

Preheat the oven to 200°C (400°F) Gas 6.

Put the breadcrumbs, chicken or turkey, egg, spring onions, ground coriander, fresh coriander, fish sauce or soy sauce and chilli sauce in a bowl.

Mix well with your hands, then roll the mixture into small balls – use about 1 tablespoon of mixture for each.

Arrange the meatballs in the prepared baking dish. Bake in the preheated oven for 25 minutes until golden brown and cooked all the way through.

Serve the meatballs straight from the baking dish with some sweet chilli sauce for dipping and some Thai fragrant rice on the side.

This gorgeous, tangy dish can be prepared in advance up to the point where it is put in the oven. The sauce around the duck, before it is put into the oven, must be very thick, because the pak-choi or cabbage gives off so much water that the dish can easily become diluted.

braised duck and ginger

4 large duck breasts, cut into thick slices

5 teaspoons cornflour

4 tablespoons yellow bean paste or sauce

2 tablespoons Shaohsing (sweet Chinese rice wine) or mirin

2 teaspoons sugar

freshly ground black pepper

1 onion, finely chopped

2 tablespoons peanut oil

10 cm fresh ginger, peeled and thickly sliced

2 garlic cloves, crushed

grated zest of 1 unwaxed orange or tangerine

2 tablespoons dark soy sauce

4 baby pak-choi, halved lengthways or ½ Chinese cabbage, sliced crossways

SERVES 4

Preheat the oven to 180°C (350°F) Gas 4.

Put the duck in a bowl, sprinkle with 1 teaspoon of the cornflour and mix until coated.

Heat a wok or frying pan, add the duck and stir-fry to release the fat and firm up the meat. Remove with a slotted spoon and return the duck to the bowl.

Put the bean paste or sauce in a small bowl, add 125ml water, the Shaohsing or mirin, sugar and freshly ground black pepper and mix well.

Add the onion to the wok or pan, then add the bean paste mixture. Simmer for about 30 seconds, then pour the mixture over the duck. Reheat the wok with the oil and sauté the ginger and garlic to release their flavour. Return the duck and its sauce to the wok, add the zest and simmer lightly until most of the water has evaporated.

Mix the remaining cornflour with 2 tablespoons water and the soy sauce, stir into the wok and bring to the boil, stirring.

Line a heavy casserole with the pak-choi or Chinese cabbage, arrange the duck over the top, then pour over the sauce. Cook in the preheated oven for 10 minutes until tender. Remove from the oven and, if the leaves have given off too much liquid, pour it into a saucepan or wok and boil until it thickens again to a coating consistency.

A healthy version of the Greek holiday favourite, this is a good dish to prepare in advance. Aubergines contain a host of vitamins and minerals and provide the perfect receptacle for the simple moussaka filling.

2 aubergines

1 teaspoon olive oil

300 g minced lamb

1 onion, finely chopped

2 garlic cloves, crushed

1 teaspoon ground cinnamon

1 teaspoon dried mint

1 tablespoon tomato purée

salad, to serve

TOPPING

150 g Greek yoghurt

1 egg yolk

freshly grated nutmeg

2 tomatoes, sliced

SERVES 4

moussaka–filled aubergines

Preheat the grill to medium.

Cut both aubergines in half lengthways and scoop out the flesh with a spoon, leaving an inner shell approximately 5 mm thick. Cut the aubergine flesh into small dice and set aside for the filling. Rub the olive oil into the aubergine shells and season the flesh lightly, then put under the preheated grill for 5–6 minutes until golden brown and slightly softened. Transfer to a baking sheet.

Preheat the oven to 200°C (400°F) Gas 6.

Put the lamb in a non-stick frying pan. Dry-fry with the onion and garlic over high heat for 5 minutes until browned. Mix in the aubergine flesh, cinnamon, mint, tomato purée and 6 tablespoons cold water, season the mixture and cook for 5 minutes.

Spoon the lamb filling into the aubergine shells. Mix the yoghurt with the egg yolk, nutmeg and seasoning, then pour this over the filling. Top with the sliced tomatoes and bake in the preheated oven for 20 minutes. Serve with a salad.

This is very simple but surprisingly effective, given how few ingredients there are, so make sure you adjust the seasoning carefully as it makes such a difference. Trim the stem end only of the okra, taking off the tiniest layer of the already-cut surface, to discourage the sticky liquid from oozing out.

greek braised lamb
with okra

3 tablespoons olive oil

4 lamb steaks, about 250 g each, cut from the leg and deboned

1 small onion, sliced

2 garlic cloves, crushed

4 tomatoes, skinned (see page 19) and deseeded

250 g okra, trimmed

sea salt and freshly ground black pepper

new potatoes, to serve

freshly chopped flat leaf parsley, to serve

SERVES 4

Preheat the oven to 180°C (350°F) Gas 4.

Heat the oil in a wide, shallow, flameproof casserole or saucepan. Season the meat, add to the pan and brown the pieces all over. Remove the meat with a slotted spoon, put on a plate and set aside in a warm place.

Add the onion and garlic to the pan and cook until softened and lightly browned. Add the tomatoes and simmer to a pulp.

Return the lamb to the pan, turn to coat, taste and adjust the seasoning and cover with a lid. Bring to the boil on top of the stove, then transfer to the preheated oven and simmer for 20 minutes.

Add the okra, cover and simmer for a further 20 minutes, removing the lid for the last 10 minutes of cooking time, to let the liquid reduce enough to just coat the meat without becoming oily. Serve with new potatoes and sprinkle with chopped parsley.

Nothing beats a classic leg of lamb for a favourite family roast. At the weekend, when you can afford to spend a little more time cooking, this is a lovely meal to prepare to get the whole family sitting round the dinner table together. Try this Italian take on the classic version – flavoured with lemon and garlic, with the salty seasoning in the gravy supplied by anchovies.

italian roast leg of lamb
with lemon and anchovy sauce

1 leg of lamb, 2.5–3 kg

2 garlic cloves, thinly sliced

1 tablespoon olive oil

175 ml white wine

sea salt and freshly ground black pepper

SAUCE

5 anchovy fillets

175 ml chicken stock

grated lemon zest from 1 unwaxed lemon

1 tablespoon freshly chopped flat leaf parsley

an instant-read thermometer

SERVES 5

Preheat the oven to 200°C (400°F) Gas 6 if you want the lamb medium rare, or 170°C (325°F) Gas 3 for well done.

Make slits in the meat in several places and insert the slivers of garlic. Brush the lamb with the oil and season all over. Set it in a roasting tin and pour the wine around. Roast in the preheated oven until an instant-read thermometer registers 63°C (145°F) for medium rare, or until the thermometer registers 77°C (170°F) for well done. It will take 1¼–2½ hours depending on the oven temperature. Baste the meat from time to time, adding water if the wine becomes low.

When the lamb is cooked to your liking, transfer it to a serving dish and leave to rest in a warm place while you make the gravy. Discard any excess fat from the roasting tin, then add the anchovies, crushing them to a paste with a fork. Stir in the stock until the anchovies have been absorbed. Add the lemon zest and parsley and any juices that have come out of the lamb during the resting period, then pour into a sauceboat to serve.

1 medium onion, coarsely chopped

4 garlic cloves, coarsely chopped

1 red pepper, halved,
deseeded and coarsely chopped

1 fresh fat red chilli,
deseeded and chopped

2 teaspoons mild chilli seasoning
(powder)

1 teaspoon sweet paprika

1 teaspoon ground cumin

1 teaspoon ground coriander

½ teaspoon ground cinnamon

1 teaspoon dried oregano

300 ml lager

500 g pork steak

4 tablespoons sunflower oil

400 g tinned chopped tomatoes

350 ml tomato juice or passata

25 g very dark chocolate, chopped

400 g tinned pinto beans or
black-eyed peas, drained and rinsed

sea salt and freshly ground
black pepper

TO SERVE

soft tortillas

tomato salsa

chopped avocado in soured cream

green rice

SERVES 4–6

mexican pork and beans
in red chilli sauce

This special version of chilli is made with pork and just a few beans, then enriched Mexican-style with a little chocolate for depth. Don't be put off by the list of ingredients. You will already have many of them in your kitchen cupboard. Serve it with salsa, chopped avocado in soured cream, warm tortillas and plenty of green rice (basmati steamed with herbs and spinach) for a great family feast. It's even better made the day before and it freezes very well.

Put the onion, garlic, red pepper, chilli, chilli seasoning, paprika, cumin, coriander, cinnamon and oregano in a food processor. Add half the lager and blend to a smooth purée.

Trim the pork steaks, then cut into large pieces. Working in batches, heat the oil in a large saucepan, add the pork and fry until browned. Transfer to a plate.

Add the purée to the pan and cook, stirring continuously, over moderate heat for 5 minutes – make sure it doesn't catch and burn, but it should start to caramelize. Stir in the remaining lager, tomatoes, tomato juice, the pork and juices. Season and bring to the boil. Reduce the heat and simmer very gently, half-covered, for 30–35 minutes until the pork is tender and the sauce thickened. Stir in the chocolate and beans and heat through.

Serve with the tortillas, salsa, chopped avocado in soured cream and green rice.

pork with leeks and mushroom sauce

two lean pork loin steaks,
125 g each

½ teaspoon olive oil

1 leek, chopped

100 g mushrooms, sliced

100 ml chicken stock

2 teaspoons wholegrain mustard

1 teaspoon cornflour blended with
a little cold water

2 tablespoons crème fraîche

sea salt and freshly ground
black pepper

roasted squash, to serve

SERVES 2

The satisfying savoury sauce is a fabulous complement to pork and it really couldn't be easier to throw together. The dish goes particularly well with roasted squash.

Lightly season the pork steaks and heat the olive oil in a non-stick frying pan. Add the pork and sauté for 4 minutes on one side, then turn, scattering the leeks around the pork. Cook for 2 minutes, then stir in the mushrooms and cook for 2 minutes. Remove the pork steaks to a plate to keep warm while you finish the sauce.

Pour the stock into the pan, mix in the mustard and boil rapidly for 3 minutes until slightly syrupy. Stir the blended cornflour into the pan and cook until the sauce has thickened slightly. Remove from the heat and stir in the crème fraîche. Spoon the sauce over the pork steaks and serve accompanied by roasted squash.

herby sausages with polenta
and rosemary, red onion and redcurrant gravy

12 good-quality herby sausages

sea salt and freshly ground black pepper

ROSEMARY, RED ONION AND REDCURRANT GRAVY

2 tablespoons olive oil

2 red onions, thinly sliced

2 fresh rosemary sprigs, broken up

2 teaspoons plain flour

2 tablespoons redcurrant jelly

300 ml red wine

300 ml beef stock

25 g butter

POLENTA

150 g powdered polenta

50 g butter

75 g Parmesan, freshly grated

SERVES 4

This is an Italian take on sausage and mash but with a bit of British redcurrant jelly thrown in because it makes onion gravy wonderfully sticky. If you've tried polenta before and weren't blown away, try it again now: the secret, as with most of the good things in life, is lots of butter, cheese and seasoning.

Put 750 ml water in a medium pan over high heat, cover and heat until it simmers.

Pour the polenta into the pan of simmering water and beat out any lumps. Reduce the heat to low and bubble away for 30 minutes or according to the manufacturer's instructions.

To make the rosemary, red onion and redcurrant gravy, heat the olive oil in a frying pan and start cooking the onions and rosemary over medium heat, stirring. When the onions are beginning to soften, reduce the heat, cover and leave to soften slowly in their own juices. After 10–15 minutes, stir in the flour and cook for about 1 minute until it is no longer pale. Add the jelly, wine and stock and bring to the boil. Leave to bubble away gently for 15 minutes while you cook the sausages.

Preheat the grill. Put the sausages on a baking sheet lined with aluminium foil and grill for 15 minutes, turning halfway through.

When everything is ready, beat the butter and Parmesan into the polenta and season. Beat the butter into the gravy and season to taste. Transfer the polenta to bowls, top with 3 sausages and pour over the hot gravy.

Spareribs make a wonderful supper dish, because they can be cooked in advance and reheated when required. Amazingly, when roasted in the oven, they are more succulent than they are when barbecued (the usual method). Because they are cooked long and slowly, they don't dry out so much.

roast sticky spareribs
marinated and glazed

12 spareribs, about 2 kg

STICKY MARINADE

2 tablespoons honey

4 tablespoons soy sauce

1 tablespoon ground ginger

1 tablespoon Dijon mustard

1 tablespoon grated fresh ginger

1 teaspoon oil

SERVES 4

To make the marinade, put the honey, soy sauce, ground ginger, mustard, fresh ginger and oil in a roasting tin and mix well. Add the ribs and turn to coat with the mixture. Set aside for several hours or overnight in the refrigerator.

Remove the tin from the refrigerator about 30 minutes before you want to start cooking, so the ribs can return to room temperature while you preheat the oven. Preheat the oven to 180°C (350°F) Gas 4.

Roast in the preheated oven for 1½ hours, turning over after 1 hour. Serve with napkins.

This recipe makes a change from ordinary mashed potatoes. Serve with roast chicken or pork and the meal is pretty much complete. Alternatively, this is useful when cooking for a mixed crowd of carnivores and vegetarians. Omit the ham and it can serve as a vegetarian main dish.

mashed potato pie with
peas, ham, cheese and chives

1 kg potatoes

1 bay leaf

1 tablespoon extra virgin olive oil

1 onion, finely chopped

100 g shelled peas, fresh or frozen and thawed

30 g unsalted butter

250 ml milk or cream (or a bit of both)

1 egg, beaten

50 g ham, sliced into thin ribbons

a small bunch of fresh chives, scissor-snipped

90 g mature Cheddar, grated

sea salt and freshly ground black pepper

a baking dish or ceramic tart mould, 24 cm in diameter, well greased

SERVES 4

Preheat the oven to 190°C (375°F) Gas 5.

Peel the potatoes and halve if large (the potatoes should all be about the same size to cook evenly). Put in a large saucepan, add water to cover, then add the bay leaf and some salt. Boil until tender, about 20 minutes.

Meanwhile, heat the oil in a frying pan, add the onion and a pinch of salt and fry until browned, 5–7 minutes. Put the peas in a microwave-proof bowl with water to cover and microwave on HIGH for 3 minutes, then drain. (Alternatively, blanch in boiling water for 3 minutes.)

Drain the cooked potatoes, then mash, mixing in the butter and milk or cream. Season with salt and stir in the egg until well blended.

Stir in the onion, peas, ham, chives and half the Cheddar. Season to taste. Transfer to the prepared dish and spread evenly. Sprinkle with the remaining Cheddar and bake in the preheated oven until well browned, 40–45 minutes. Serve hot or warm.

This is a gentle, aromatic meat curry from Indonesia made all in one pot with cubed beef. Tamarind purée is sold in small jars in supermarkets and Asian stores. Serve with Thai fragrant rice and green beans.

500 g braising steak, cubed

1 tablespoon tamarind purée

1 cinnamon stick

1 tablespoon dark muscovado sugar

2 tablespoons soy sauce

250 ml unsalted beef or vegetable stock

¼ teaspoon ground black pepper

¼ teaspoon freshly grated nutmeg

seeds from 6 cardamom pods, crushed

2 medium red onions, quartered

3 garlic cloves, roughly chopped

3 cm fresh ginger, peeled and roughly chopped

Thai fragrant rice, to serve

green beans, to serve

SERVES 4

beef rendang

Put the meat in a heavy medium saucepan or casserole dish. Add the tamarind, cinnamon stick, sugar, soy sauce, stock, pepper, nutmeg and cardamom seeds.

Put the onions, garlic and ginger in a food processor and blend until very finely chopped. Spoon into the saucepan with the rest of the ingredients and set over medium heat. Bring the mixture to the boil, stir gently to make sure everything is well combined, then cover with a lid.

Turn the heat right down and leave to simmer very gently for 1½ hours, stirring now and then. Remove the lid and cook uncovered for a further 20–30 minutes until the sauce is very thick. Remove the cinnamon stick and serve.

home-made burgers

600 g lean minced beef
1 garlic clove, crushed
1 shallot, finely diced
a handful of fresh parsley, chopped
1 teaspoon Worcestershire sauce
olive oil, for frying
4 streaky bacon rashers
4 ciabatta rolls
4 tablespoons mayonnaise
4 slices of beef tomato
100 g Cheddar, grated (optional)
1 avocado, sliced
4 iceberg lettuce leaves, shredded
sea salt and freshly ground
black pepper
ketchup and mustard, to serve

MAKES 4

Burgers are fantastically versatile, so build yours just as you wish, with or without the garnishes suggested below.

Preheat the grill to medium.

Put the minced beef, garlic, shallot, parsley and Worcestershire sauce in a large bowl, season and mix well with your hands. Divide the mixture into 4 and shape into burgers.

Heat some oil in a large frying pan and cook the burgers for 2 minutes on each side for rare, 3 minutes for medium-rare and 4 minutes for well done.

Meanwhile, grill the bacon under the preheated grill until crisp. Cut the ciabatta rolls in half and grill the insides, then spread with mayonnaise. Put a slice of tomato on the grilled base and a burger on top, followed by a handful of Cheddar, if using, a bacon rasher, a slice or two of avocado and some lettuce. Sandwich together with the remaining bread and serve with ketchup and mustard.

Steak and melting, gooey blue cheese are a match made in heaven. This recipe uses mature Stilton, but you could equally well use Gorgonzola.

toasted steak, stilton and watercress sandwich

60 g mature blue Stilton, rind removed

25 g butter, softened

a small pinch of cayenne pepper or paprika

two 225-g thinly sliced minute steaks

1 tablespoon olive oil

1 medium ciabatta loaf

a small handful of watercress

sea salt and freshly ground black pepper

BALSAMIC DRESSING

1 teaspoon balsamic vinegar

3 teaspoons light olive oil

a ridged stove-top grill pan (optional)

SERVES 2

Preheat the grill to hot.

To make the balsamic dressing, mix the vinegar and olive oil and some seasoning in a small bowl. Set aside.

Mash the Stilton with the butter and season with the cayenne pepper. Heat a ridged stove-top grill pan or a frying pan over high heat until very hot. Rub the slices of steak lightly with the olive oil and season. Sear for 1 minute each side, then set aside.

Cut the ciabatta in half crossways, then in half lengthways. Briefly toast the outside of the bottom halves under the preheated grill, then turn them over and pile on the steak slices and dot with the Stilton butter. Grill for about 1 minute until the cheese melts, then transfer to warm plates.

Lightly toast the outside of the remaining halves of ciabatta. Place a few watercress leaves on top of the Stilton butter and drizzle with the balsamic dressing, then cover with the remaining ciabatta halves. Serve immediately.

a fabulous paella

3 tablespoons good olive oil

6 chicken thighs

175 g chorizo, cut into chunks

2 garlic cloves, finely chopped

1 large onion, finely chopped

1 large red pepper, deseeded and finely sliced

500 g Spanish paella rice

175 ml dry white wine

a good pinch of dried red chilli flakes

2 teaspoons sweet Spanish paprika

about 1.2 litres chicken stock

a large pinch of saffron threads, soaked in 3 tablespoons hot water

6 ripe tomatoes, quartered

12 uncooked prawns, shells on

500 g fresh mussels, scrubbed, rinsed and debearded

125 g fresh or frozen peas

4 tablespoons freshly chopped flat leaf parsley

sea salt and freshly ground black pepper

wedges of lime or lemon, to serve

SERVES 6

Paella is the perfect dish for summer parties – everything can be prepared ahead of time, then you just add the ingredients in a steady stream until the whole thing comes together. But in fact, this paella is ready quite quickly so it's equally good for a mid-week treat. The smell alone is wonderfully enticing, so make enough for seconds.

Heat the olive oil in a paella pan or large, deep frying pan. Add the chicken thighs and chorizo and brown all over, turning frequently. Stir in the garlic, onion and red pepper and cook for about 5 minutes until softened.

Stir in the rice until all the grains are coated and glossy. Add the wine and leave it to bubble and reduce until almost disappeared. Stir in the chilli flakes, paprika, chicken stock and soaked saffron. Stir well, bring to the boil and simmer gently for 10 minutes.

Stir in the tomatoes and prawns and cook gently for 5 minutes before finally tucking the mussels into the rice and adding the peas. Cook for another 5 minutes until the mussels open (take out any that do not open after this time). At this stage, almost all the liquid will have been absorbed and the rice will be tender.

Sprinkle the chopped parsley over the top and serve immediately, straight from the pan with a big pile of lime or lemon wedges on the side. Serve with napkins.

fish pie

500 ml milk

750 g smoked or fresh haddock, skinned

275 g unsalted butter

1 tablespoon English mustard powder

4 tablespoons plain flour

2 hard-boiled eggs, peeled and quartered

1 kg floury potatoes

sea salt and freshly ground black pepper

SERVES 4

If traditional fish pie conjures up memories of stodgy school dinners, think again! This delicious recipe is a winner on a cold evening and the mustard in the sauce provides a special flavour that you can't quite put your finger on.

Preheat the oven to 200°C (400°F) Gas 6.

Put the milk in a wide saucepan, heat just to boiling point, then add the fish. Turn off the heat and leave the fish to poach until opaque – do not allow it to over-cook.

Meanwhile, melt 125 g of the butter in another saucepan, then stir in the mustard and flour. Remove from the heat and strain the poaching liquid into the pan.

Arrange the fish and eggs in a shallow pie dish or casserole.

Return the pan to the heat and, whisking vigorously to smooth out any lumps, bring the mixture to the boil. Season to taste. (Take care: if you are using smoked fish, it may be salty enough.) Pour the sauce into the casserole and mix carefully with the fish and eggs.

Cook the potatoes in salted boiling water until soft, then drain. Return to the pan. Melt the remaining butter in a small saucepan. Reserve 4 tablespoons of this butter and stir the remainder into the potatoes. Mash well and season. Spoon the mixture carefully over the sauced fish, brush with the reserved butter and transfer to the oven. Cook for 20 minutes, or until nicely browned.

mediterranean chunky fish stew with cheese toasts

1 small onion, finely chopped

2 garlic cloves:
1 crushed and 1 halved

a pinch of dried thyme

125 g fennel (hard core removed),
finely chopped

1 tablespoon olive oil

50 ml Noilly Prat, dry Martini or
dry white wine

400 g passata

a pinch of saffron threads

freshly squeezed juice and grated
zest of 1 unwaxed orange

200 g skinless cod fillet,
cut into large chunks

4 thin slices of baguette

50 g Emmental or Gruyère
cheese, grated

sea salt and freshly ground
black pepper

SERVES 2

If you have ever tasted the classic French fish soup bouillabaisse *and enjoyed the flavour, then this is a good cheat's version. The combination of saffron, orange and fennel gives the stew its distinctive flavour. If you can't find Noilly Prat, use dry Martini or a dry white wine in its place. If you have time to make the base of the stew the day before you plan to eat it, the flavours will develop even further – simply cook the fish at the last moment.*

Heat the olive oil in a large pan, then gently sauté the onion, crushed garlic, thyme and fennel for about 6–8 minutes or until soft. Add the Noilly Prat, dry Martini or dry white wine and leave to bubble, uncovered, until the liquid has almost reduced to nothing.

Add the passata, saffron, orange juice and zest and 200 ml cold water. Raise the heat and cook for 10 minutes. Add the cod and cook gently for a further 2 minutes, then season to taste.

Meanwhile, preheat the grill to high. Toast the baguette slices on each side under the grill until lightly golden. Rub the halved garlic over each slice and sprinkle with the grated cheese.

Ladle the stew into warmed deep serving bowls and balance the cheese-topped toasts on top. Serve immediately.

2 tablespoons vegetable oil

1 onion, grated

3 garlic cloves, crushed

5 cm fresh ginger,
peeled and sliced

1 mild red chilli, chopped

1 teaspoon turmeric

2 teaspoons curry powder

1 teaspoon ground coriander

1 teaspoon ground cumin

400 g frozen cooked shelled
prawns, defrosted

a 400-g tin chopped tomatoes

freshly squeezed juice of 2 limes

a handful of fresh coriander,
chopped

sea salt and freshly ground
black pepper

basmati rice, to serve

SERVES 4

Tiger prawns or large peeled prawns are ideal for this colourful, citrus-flavoured curry. You really can't find a faster, easier one-bowl meal than this – or with tastier results. Serve with basmati.

prawn curry

Heat the oil in a large pan, add the onion, garlic, ginger and chilli and cook for 5 minutes over medium heat. Add the turmeric, curry powder, ground coriander and cumin and mix well. Add the prawns and cook for 3 minutes.

Pour in the tomatoes and lime juice, season and bring to the boil. Reduce the heat and simmer for 5 minutes. Add the chopped coriander and serve with basmati rice.

easy tuna fish cakes

600 g sweet potatoes,
peeled and chopped

300 g cooked or tinned tuna,
coarsely flaked

2 spring onions, chopped

1 egg

100 g powdered polenta

3 tablespoons olive oil

sea salt and freshly ground
black pepper

1 lemon, to serve

tomato salad, to serve

SERVES 4

Polenta is cornmeal, and it makes a lovely crumb coating on these fish cakes. If using tinned tuna, buy a good-quality brand that has a dense texture and large chunks. Alternatively, pan-cook fresh tuna and flake it yourself.

Cook the sweet potatoes in a pan of simmering water for 20 minutes. Drain well and mash. Add the tuna, spring onions and egg, season and mix well. Divide the mixture into 8 equal pieces and shape into patties.

Put the polenta on a plate and dip the fish cakes in it until coated on all sides.

Heat the olive oil in a frying pan and fry the fish cakes on each side until golden. Serve with lemon wedges and a tomato salad.

tuna and potato stew

1 small red pepper

1 small yellow pepper

1 small green pepper

3 tablespoons extra virgin olive oil

1 large onion, finely chopped

2 garlic cloves, finely chopped

5 tomatoes, skinned, deseeded and chopped (reserve any juices)

½ teaspoon sweet paprika

1 bay leaf

500 g potatoes, peeled and cut into 1-cm slices

2 slices of fresh tuna, 500 g each, cut into 6 chunky pieces each

2 tablespoons freshly torn parsley leaves

coarse sea salt and freshly ground black pepper

FRIED BREAD

6 slices of white bread, cut into triangles

extra virgin olive oil, for frying

SERVES 4–6

This is a stew from the Basque region, where fishermen used to make it on board their boats, using bonito or albacore tuna from the Bay of Biscay, and mopping up the soupy juices with lots of delicious fried bread.

Halve and deseed the red, yellow and green peppers and cut the flesh into 1-cm cubes.

Heat the oil in a heatproof casserole, add the onion, garlic and peppers and fry over low heat until softened but not coloured, 12–15 minutes. Increase the heat and stir in the tomatoes and their juice. When the mixture starts to thicken, add the paprika, bay leaf and some seasoning.

Stir in the potatoes and 400 ml boiling water and simmer gently for about 15 minutes until the potatoes are cooked.

Meanwhile, to make the fried bread, heat the olive oil in a large frying pan, add the triangles of bread and fry on both sides until golden. Remove and drain on kitchen paper.

Season the pieces of tuna 10 minutes before cooking. Add the tuna to the casserole and after about 30 seconds, when the underside turns pale, turn the pieces over and turn off the heat. Leave for 5 minutes. Sprinkle with parsley and serve with the triangles of fried bread.

pan-fried salmon
with cannellini bean purée

75 g rocket

100 g baby spinach leaves, lightly rinsed

50 g watercress

16 cherry tomatoes, halved

4 boneless salmon fillets, about 200 g each

1 tablespoon olive oil

4 garlic cloves, halved

balsamic vinegar, for drizzling

sea salt and freshly ground black pepper

CANNELLINI BEAN PURÉE

400 g tinned cannellini beans, drained and rinsed

1 garlic clove, crushed

1½ tablespoons freshly squeezed lemon juice

2 tablespoons freshly chopped thyme

2 teaspoons olive oil

SERVES 4

Who says you have to eat salmon with rice, potatoes or pasta? This novel, tasty and rather sophisticated recipe uses nutritious beans instead.

Reserve a few rocket leaves for serving then put the remaining rocket, spinach and watercress in a salad bowl. Add the cherry tomatoes and set aside.

To make the cannellini bean purée, put the beans, garlic, lemon juice, thyme, oil and 2 tablespoons water in a food processor or blender. Season to taste, then process to a smooth, soft purée. Add a little more water, if necessary. Transfer to a saucepan and heat gently for about 5 minutes, stirring frequently, until piping hot. Alternatively, put the purée in a microwaveable bowl, cover and cook on HIGH for about 4 minutes, stirring halfway through, until piping hot. Leave to stand for 1 minute before serving.

Meanwhile, to cook the salmon fillets, heat the oil in a non-stick frying pan. Add the garlic and fry gently for 1 minute. Add the salmon and cook for 5–8 minutes, turning once halfway through.

Drizzle the salad with a little balsamic vinegar, season to taste and toss well. Put a spoonful of cannellini bean purée on each of 4 warmed serving plates. Put the reserved rocket leaves on top, followed by the salmon. Drizzle with a little extra virgin olive oil. Serve immediately with the salad.

Variation The bean purée would be delicious with most grilled foods. Try chicken, turkey, large prawns or tuna. Use other beans or a mixture of two or three types and keep the purée slightly chunky, if you prefer.

herb-crusted plaice and tomatoes

2 slices of seeded wholemeal bread

grated zest and freshly squeezed juice of ½ unwaxed lemon

15 g Parmesan, freshly grated

2 tablespoons freshly chopped parsley

1 tablespoon freshly chopped thyme

1 tablespoon olive oil

four plaice fillets, or other flat white fish fillets, such as lemon sole, 100 g each

4 ripe tomatoes, halved

sea salt and freshly ground black pepper

SERVES 4

This quick and easy fish supper is full of flavour. Serve with sprouting broccoli and small new potatoes.

Preheat the grill to medium and grease a baking sheet.

Process the bread to crumbs in a food processor, then mix in the lemon zest and juice, Parmesan and herbs. Add the olive oil to bind the mixture together slightly, and season lightly.

Lay out the plaice fillets and tomato halves (cut-side up) on the prepared baking sheet. Press the herby crumb mixture firmly onto the fish and tomatoes. Put under the preheated grill and cook for about 5 minutes until the crust is golden brown and the fish is cooked through. Serve immediately.

If you have a stovetop-to-oven pan, this dish can be cooked all in one pot. Use chunks of white fish such as monkfish, hake, snapper or bass and choose large, waxy salad potatoes, which won't break up on cooking.

fish baked with lemon, oregano and potatoes

125 ml extra virgin olive oil

2 onions, halved and thinly sliced

2 garlic cloves, chopped

1–2 pinches of dried red chilli flakes

1 teaspoon coriander seeds, crushed

½ teaspoon dried oregano

750 g waxy potatoes, peeled and cut into wedges

2 bay leaves

5 tablespoons white wine or vermouth

½ teaspoon grated lemon zest

700–750 g white fish (on or off the bone), cut into large chunks or steaks

2 small lemons, halved

1 tablespoon freshly chopped oregano

1 tablespoon freshly chopped flat leaf parsley

sea salt and freshly ground black pepper

SERVES 4

Preheat the oven to 200°C (400°F) Gas 6.

Heat a large frying pan or ovenproof lidded skillet over medium heat and add the oil. Add the onion and fry for 2–3 minutes, then turn the heat right down. Add 1–2 pinches of salt, cover and leave the onion to cook very gently for 10–12 minutes until soft and golden yellow. Add the garlic, chilli flakes, crushed coriander seeds and dried oregano. Cook for another 3–4 minutes.

Add the potatoes and bay leaves to the pan, turning them in the oily onions. Season generously. Cook for a few minutes, then add the wine and lemon zest. When it bubbles, cover and cook gently for 15–20 minutes or until the potatoes are just tender.

Transfer the potatoes to a large ovenproof baking dish, if necessary. Season the fish with a little salt, then nestle into the potatoes. Squeeze a little lemon juice from one of the lemon halves over the fish and spoon over a little of the oily juices. Add the lemon halves to the dish and turn in the oil.

Bake, uncovered, in the preheated oven for 20–25 minutes, basting once or twice, until the potatoes are tender and the fish cooked through. Serve sprinkled with fresh oregano and parsley.

DESSERTS & SWEET TREATS

You can't go wrong with crumble, and this simple plum crumble is a great favourite with children, especially when made with Victoria plums. Plums have such a rich flavour when they are cooked that they need little or no other flavourings. Experiment with greengages, mirabelles or yellow plums.

8–10 ripe plums

4–5 tablespoons sugar

cream, to serve

CRUMBLE TOPPING

175 g plain flour

75 g unsalted butter, chilled

a pinch of salt

50 g caster sugar

a medium, shallow, ovenproof dish

SERVES 4–6

simple plum crumble

Preheat the oven to 180°C (350°F) Gas 4 and set a baking sheet on the middle shelf to heat.

Halve the plums and remove the stones. Cut the halves into quarters if they are very large. Toss them with the sugar and tip them into the ovenproof dish.

To make the topping, put the flour, butter and salt in a bowl and rub together with your fingertips until the mixture resembles breadcrumbs. Stir in the sugar. (At this point the mixture can be popped in a plastic bag and chilled until ready to cook.)

Lightly scatter the topping mixture over the plums. Place the dish on the baking sheet in the preheated oven and bake for 40–45 minutes, until golden brown. Serve with cream.

almond fruit crumble

600 g fruit

50 g light brown sugar

custard, cream or ice cream, to serve

CRUMBLE TOPPING

125 g self-raising flour

1 teaspoon baking powder

125 g unsalted butter, diced

50 g caster sugar

50 g ground almonds

50 g rolled oats

a 1-litre ovenproof dish, greased

SERVES 4

Any combination of fruits would sit well under this toasty, crunchy, almondy crumble. Try rhubarb and ginger, apple and apricot, pear and blackcurrant or whatever's in the fruit bowl.

Preheat the oven to 190°C (375°F) Gas 5.

Put the fruit in the prepared ovenproof dish and add the brown sugar and 100 ml water.

To make the topping, put the flour, baking powder and butter in a bowl and rub together with your fingertips until the mixture resembles coarse breadcrumbs. Stir in the caster sugar, almonds and oats.

Lightly scatter the topping mixture over the fruit. Bake in the preheated oven for 30 minutes. The crumble should be golden and the fruit bubbling up around the edges. Serve with custard, cream or ice cream.

buttered apricot betty

675 g fresh apricots or
three 400-g tins apricots
in natural juice

150 g fresh breadcrumbs,
lightly toasted

100 g unsalted butter, diced

2 tablespoons golden syrup

100 ml freshly squeezed
orange juice

50 g caster sugar

cream, to serve

*a medium, ovenproof,
deep pie dish, greased*

a large roasting tin

SERVES 4

*If you have the patience, you can crack the apricot
stones and take out the kernels inside. These are very
like bitter almonds, and are a fantastic addition
when chopped and toasted with the breadcrumbs.*

Preheat the oven to 190°C (375°F) Gas 5.

Halve the fresh apricots and flip out the stones, or drain the tinned
apricots and pat dry. Place a layer of apricots in the prepared pie dish.

Reserve 4–6 tablespoons of the breadcrumbs for the top. Sprinkle
some of the rest of the breadcrumbs over the apricots, and dot with
some of the butter. Put in some more apricots and repeat these
alternate casual layers until all the apricots and breadcrumbs are
used up. Use the reserved breadcrumbs for the final top layer.

Warm the syrup with the orange juice, and pour this over the top.
Sprinkle with sugar and dot with the remaining butter.

Place the pie dish in the roasting tin and pour in enough boiling water
to come halfway up the sides of the dish. (This is a *bain-marie*.) Bake
in the preheated oven for 45 minutes, or until the apricots are soft
and the top crispy and brown. Serve warm, not hot, with cream.

This is a gorgeously moist, tangy treat to satisfy a sweet tooth after a light meal, and it is special enough to serve when you have guests, too. Polenta is a useful ingredient which gives cakes a slightly coarser, crunchier texture than wheat flour.

lemon polenta cake

175 g unsalted butter, softened

175 g unrefined caster sugar

100 g powdered polenta

½ teaspoon baking powder

175 g ground almonds

grated zest and freshly squeezed juice of 1 unwaxed lemon

½ teaspoon vanilla extract

3 eggs

crème fraîche, to serve

SYRUP

grated zest and freshly squeezed juice of 2 unwaxed lemons

50 g unrefined caster sugar

a springform cake tin, 24 cm in diameter, lightly greased

SERVES 6–8

Preheat the oven to 180°C (350°F) Gas 4.

Beat together the butter and sugar until creamy. Add the polenta, baking powder, ground almonds, lemon zest and juice, vanilla extract and eggs. Mix together until smooth.

Spoon the mixture into the prepared tin and bake in the middle of the preheated oven for 30 minutes.

Meanwhile, make the syrup. Put the lemon zest and juice in a small saucepan with the sugar and 2 tablespoons water. Bring to the boil and simmer for 2 minutes. When the cake is done, leave to cool slightly in the tin, then turn out and pierce all over with a fine skewer. Spoon the syrup over the cake, then set aside for 20 minutes while it is absorbed. Serve with crème fraîche.

It's easy to think your brownies aren't cooked and to give them those extra few minutes, which can dry them out and turn them into a mealy chocolate cake. So be brave: if the mixture doesn't wobble in the middle and a skewer inserted in the centre comes out chocolatey, remove the brownies from the oven and by the time they have cooled, they will be perfect.

chocolate brownies with
vanilla-flecked crème fraîche

250 g plain chocolate, broken into pieces, plus extra to serve

250 g unsalted butter, softened

4 large eggs, beaten

325 g golden caster sugar

½ teaspoon fine salt

125 g self-raising flour

25 g cocoa powder

200 g crème fraîche

1 vanilla pod, cut lengthways

a cake tin, 20 x 30 cm, greased and lined with greaseproof paper

MAKES 16

Preheat the oven to 180°C (350°F) Gas 4. Don't use a fan oven if you have the choice, as it dries the outside of the brownies.

Put the chocolate and butter in a heatproof bowl set over a pan of simmering water and leave for several minutes until melted, then remove from the pan and leave to cool.

Whisk together the eggs and the sugar with an electric whisk. Pour in the cooled chocolate mixture, then add the salt and finally the flour. Whisk until well blended. Pour the mixture into the prepared cake tin and bake in the centre of the preheated oven for 23–25 minutes (you have to be precise with brownies!). The outside should look crackled and the inside feel firm to the touch but will be gooey underneath. Remove from the oven and leave to cool in the tin for 15 minutes, then slice into squares.

Mix the crème fraîche with the vanilla seeds scraped from the pod and serve with a brownie square or two. Grate some extra chocolate over the top.

This really is nursery food at its most comforting. This French version uses the double rice-cooking method – blanching the rice first removes much of the starch. The result is light and delicate, not blobby and glutinous like some puddings. Serve it with red fruit coulis, chocolate sauce, cranberry sauce or custard. Of course, it's also very nice just as it is.

rice pudding

125 g risotto rice, such as arborio

500 ml whole milk, boiled

60 g sugar

1 vanilla pod, cut lengthways

15 g unsalted butter

a pinch of salt

SERVES 4

Preheat the oven to 180°C (350°F) Gas 6.

Put the rice in a saucepan and add cold water to cover. Slowly bring to the boil over medium heat, then boil for 5 minutes. Drain the rice and rinse under cold water. Set aside to drain well.

Meanwhile, put the milk in an ovenproof pan with a lid and bring to the boil. Add the sugar and vanilla pod. Remove from the heat, cover and set aside for 15 minutes. Scrape the vanilla seeds from the pod and stir them through the milk.

Add the rice to the milk, then add the butter and salt. Bring slowly to the boil. Cover and transfer to the preheated oven. Do not stir. Cook until the rice is tender and the liquid is almost completely absorbed but not dry, about 25–35 minutes. Serve warm.

The tartness and spiciness of the apples here cuts through the sweet, buttery toffee sauce. Sticky toffee sauce is very versatile and can be served with ice cream or spooned over other baked fruit, such as bananas, pears, peaches or apricots. The apples can be prepared in the morning and popped into the oven as soon as you get home.

cream or vanilla ice cream, to serve

STICKY TOFFEE SAUCE

75 g unsalted butter

75 g soft dark brown sugar

5 tablespoons double cream

STUFFED APPLES

50 g dried dates, roughly chopped

15 g stem ginger in syrup, drained and finely chopped

25 g walnuts or pecan nuts, roughly chopped

4 large cooking apples, such as Bramley or Russet, cored

SERVES 4

baked apples with dates and sticky toffee sauce

Preheat the oven to 150°C (300°F) Gas 2.

First make the sticky toffee sauce. Put the butter, sugar and cream in a pan over low heat until melted. Bring to the boil and cook for 1 minute. Remove from the heat and set aside.

To make the stuffed apples, mix together the dates, ginger and walnuts or pecan nuts. Stuff half this mixture into the cored apples and stir the remainder into the toffee sauce.

Arrange the stuffed apples in an ovenproof dish or roasting tin so that they fit tightly. Pour the toffee sauce over the apples and cover the entire dish or tin with aluminium foil.

Bake in the preheated oven for 25–30 minutes, basting the apples with the sauce occasionally. Remove the dish or tin from the oven and leave the apples to cool for 2 minutes. Serve whilst still warm, with cream or vanilla ice cream.

bread and butter puddings

300 ml milk

300 ml double cream

½ teaspoon vanilla extract

4 tablespoons caster sugar

3 eggs

6 tea cakes or hot cross buns, halved

50 g sultanas

freshly grated nutmeg, to sprinkle

6 ramekins, 200 ml each, well greased

SERVES 6

This is unbeatable comfort food. Made with tea cakes or hot cross buns for extra flavour, these individual puddings cook in under 20 minutes.

Preheat the oven to 180°C (350°F) Gas 4.

Put the milk, cream, vanilla extract and 3 tablespoons of the sugar into a saucepan and heat until the sugar dissolves.

Put the eggs into a bowl and whisk well. Stir in 2–3 tablespoons of the hot milk mixture to warm the eggs, then stir in the remainder of the hot milk. You should have a custard-like mixture.

Lightly toast the tea cakes or hot cross buns and cut into quarters. Divide between the prepared ramekins and sprinkle with the sultanas.

Pour in the custard, grate a little nutmeg over the top, then sprinkle with the remaining sugar. Bake in the preheated oven for 18–20 minutes until firm. Leave to cool a little, then serve warm.

This is a very simple recipe, a bit like a frangipane and fruit tart, but without the fuss of pastry making. They must be eaten soon after baking, but the almond filling can be made several hours in advance and refrigerated until needed, and you can hollow out the peaches at the same time. If you don't have a muffin tin, make little rings out of foil to keep the peaches upright while baking.

3 tablespoons unsalted butter, at room temperature

3 tablespoons caster sugar

1 large egg

40 g ground almonds

30 g finely crushed amaretti biscuits

6 ripe peaches

Greek yoghurt or crème fraîche, to serve

RASPBERRY SAUCE

250 g fresh raspberries (or frozen and thawed)

1 tablespoon icing sugar

1 tablespoon freshly squeezed lemon juice

a 12-hole muffin tin

SERVES 6

baked amaretti peaches
with raspberry sauce

Preheat the oven to 180°C (350°F) Gas 4.

Put the butter and sugar in a bowl and beat until blended. Beat in the egg. Stir in the ground almonds and amaretti until well mixed. Set aside.

Cut the peaches in half and remove the stones. Using a small spoon, scrape out a bit more from each hollow to make more space for the filling (not too much). Divide the filling between the peaches, spooning some into each hollow. Put a peach half into each muffin hole to keep them upright while baking.

Bake in the preheated oven until the filling is puffed and golden, about 25–30 minutes.

Meanwhile, to make the sauce, put the raspberries, icing sugar and lemon juice in a small food processor and purée. Set aside.

Serve the peaches warm with the raspberry sauce.

double chocolate muffins

250 g plain flour

40 g cocoa powder

2 teaspoons baking powder

100 g caster sugar

80 g chocolate chips,
plus extra to sprinkle

2 large eggs

230 ml milk

125 ml sunflower oil

1 teaspoon vanilla extract

*a 12-hole muffin tin,
lined with paper cases*

MAKES 12

Everybody loves chocolate muffins! These are quick to prepare and made with cocoa powder plus chocolate chips for maximum chocolate flavour.

Preheat the oven to 200°C (400°F) Gas 6.

Set a large sieve over a large bowl. Tip the flour, cocoa, baking powder and sugar into the sieve and sift into the bowl. Add the chocolate chips.

Break the eggs into a second bowl. Add the milk, oil and vanilla extract, then mix well with a fork. Add the flour mixture and gently stir with a wooden spoon.

Spoon the mixture into the paper cases – each one should be about half full. Sprinkle with extra chocolate chips.

Bake in the preheated oven for about 20 minutes until well-risen and just firm. Remove from the oven and turn the muffins out onto a wire rack to cool for about 30 minutes. These muffins are best eaten the same day.

This delightfully fresh-tasting pudding is based on a traditional British recipe. Served warm (it's best that way), the bottom layer forms a tangy, lemony sauce for the light sponge layer, but it is also delicious cold (see Variation), when the sauce sets into a light custard that is lovely with the taste of blackberries. So there you are – two recipes for the price of one!

lemon and blackberry puddings

200–250 g ripe blackberries

100 g caster sugar,
plus 1 tablespoon

4 tablespoons butter, softened

1 vanilla pod, cut lengthways

grated zest and freshly squeezed
juice of 1 large unwaxed lemon

2 large eggs, separated

2 slightly heaped tablespoons
plain flour

250 ml milk

4 tablespoons single cream,
plus extra to serve (optional)

½ teaspoon cream of tartar

4–5 small ovenproof dishes, greased

SERVES 4–5

Preheat the oven to 180°C (350°F) Gas 4.

Put the blackberries and the 1 tablespoon sugar in a bowl, toss gently, then spoon into the dishes.

Put the butter and the remaining sugar in a bowl and beat until creamy. Scrape the seeds from the vanilla pod into the mixture and beat to mix. Beat in the lemon zest, followed by the egg yolks. Sift in the flour, stir in, then gradually beat in the milk, cream and lemon juice.

Put the egg whites and cream of tartar in a separate, grease-free bowl and whisk until stiff but not dry. Beat 2 tablespoons of the egg whites into the pudding mixture, then fold in the remainder with a spatula. Spoon the mixture into the prepared dishes and bake in the preheated oven for 30–35 minutes. Serve hot or warm, with cream, if you like.

Variation To serve cold, bake in a 1-litre shallow ovenproof dish for an additional 5–10 minutes. Leave to cool, then chill. Whisk 200 ml whipping cream and 2 tablespoons vanilla sugar in a bowl until thick. Spread over the pudding, then decorate with blackberries and lemon zest.

yoghurt cake

a pot of natural set yoghurt

2 pots of sugar

3 pots of flour

2 eggs

1 tablespoon sunflower oil

1 teaspoon bicarbonate of soda

a pinch of salt

freshly squeezed juice of 1 orange

1 tablespoon icing sugar,
to decorate

*a deep cake tin, 23 cm in diameter,
greased*

SERVES 8

This is such a simple cake that there's no excuse not to serve it up for dessert. The yoghurt pot is the measure, so it doesn't really matter what size you use. Plain, French-style set yoghurt works well. If you don't fancy orange, try other flavourings: cinnamon, honey, vanilla, chocolate, fruit pieces, etc. This is great to make, and eat, with children.

Preheat the oven to 180°C (350°F) Gas 4.

Empty the yoghurt into a large bowl and wipe out the pot so when you measure the other ingredients, they won't stick. Add the sugar, flour, eggs, oil, bicarbonate of soda, salt and half the orange juice. Stir well.

Pour into the prepared cake tin and bake in the preheated oven until a knife inserted in the middle comes out clean, about 15–20 minutes. Remove from the oven and pierce a few holes in the top with a fork. Pour over the remaining orange juice. Leave to cool slightly, then turn out onto a wire rack to cool. Dust with icing sugar and serve at room temperature.

Sweet, sticky and indulgent, these little plum fudge puddings can be prepared in advance, then cooked just before serving. Making them in individual ramekins means they look special enough to serve up at a dinner party, too.

50 g unsalted butter

50 g honey

2 tablespoons double cream

2 tablespoons soft brown sugar

1 teaspoon ground mixed spice

75 g fresh white breadcrumbs

2 ripe plums, halved, stoned and thinly sliced

crème fraîche, to serve

4 ramekins, 150 ml each

SERVES 4

plum fudge puddings

Preheat the oven to 200°C (400°F) Gas 6.

Put the butter, honey and cream in a saucepan and heat until melted. Put the sugar, mixed spice and breadcrumbs in a bowl and stir well.

Divide half the buttery fudge mixture between the ramekin dishes and top with a layer of plum slices and half the breadcrumb mix. Add the remaining plums and breadcrumbs, then spoon over the remaining sauce.

Put the ramekins on a baking sheet and bake in the preheated oven for 20 minutes. Remove from the oven and leave to cool for 5 minutes, then carefully unmould the puddings and serve with a spoonful of crème fraîche.

raspberry and ginger tiramisu

150 g raspberries

2 teaspoons caster sugar

130 g sponge fingers
(savoiardi biscuits)

125 ml cooled, strong black coffee,
such as espresso

75 ml coffee-flavoured liqueur,
such as Tia Maria or Kahlúa, or a
cream liqueur, such as Baileys

250 g mascarpone cheese

50 g icing sugar

1 teaspoon ground ginger

1 tablespoon milk

cocoa powder, for dusting

a few pinches of ground cinnamon

*4 glass sundae dishes, Martini glasses
or large wine glasses*

SERVES 4

This quick and easy recipe is a winner when you've got friends coming over for supper straight after work, as it can be assembled in the morning and left in the fridge to improve during the day. It's useful to always keep a packet of sponge fingers in the cupboard and a tub of mascarpone in the fridge for occasions such as these. A strong black freshly made espresso will give you a more intense and authentic flavour, but you can use an instant coffee (made fairly strong), if preferred.

Put the raspberries in a bowl, add the caster sugar and lightly mash with a fork. Spoon the fruit into the sundae dishes, Martini glasses or large wine glasses.

Pour the coffee and liqueur into a small bowl and mix together. Dip both ends of the sponge fingers in the coffee mixture so that they absorb the liquid and darken in colour, then put them on top of the raspberries. Use your fingers to press the sponge down a little to fit the glass.

Put the mascarpone, icing sugar and ginger in a large bowl and beat to combine. Gradually beat in the milk to form a smooth, creamy mixture. Spoon this mixture over the sponge fingers. Dust with a little cocoa powder and sprinkle a pinch of cinnamon over each glass.

Serve immediately or refrigerate until ready to serve.

Variation You could use amaretti biscuits instead of the sponge fingers. They give the pudding a lovely almond flavour.

This is a wonderful way of cooking pears. It is so simple to make, but tastes very luxurious. Choose pears that are ripe but not too soft, or they will overcook in the oven. If you can't get a good rich Marsala or Vin Santo, use sweet sherry or Madeira instead.

caramelized pears with
marsala and mascarpone cream

6 large ripe pears

150 g caster sugar

150 ml Marsala or Vin Santo

200 g mascarpone cheese

1 vanilla pod, cut lengthways

a flameproof, ovenproof pan or dish

SERVES 6

Preheat the oven to 190°C (375°F) Gas 5.

Cut the pears in half and scoop out the cores – do not peel them. Sprinkle the sugar into the pan or dish. Set over medium heat and leave the sugar to melt and caramelize. Remove from the heat as soon as it reaches a medium-brown colour and quickly arrange the pears cut-side down in the caramel.

Bake in the preheated oven until the pears are soft, 20–25 minutes. Carefully lift out the pears and transfer to an ovenproof serving dish, keeping the caramel in the pan.

Put the pan on top of the stove over medium heat and add the Marsala or Vin Santo. Bring to the boil, stirring to dislodge any set caramel, and boil fast until reduced and syrupy. Set aside.

Scoop out a good teaspoon from each cooked pear and put it in a bowl. Add the mascarpone and the seeds scraped from the vanilla pod and beat well. Fill the centres of the pears with the mascarpone mixture. Return to the oven for 5 minutes until it has heated through. Serve with the caramel sauce spooned over the top.

cheat's cherry brûlée

300 g ripe cherries, stoned

100 ml cream or crème fraîche

100 ml fromage frais

1 teaspoon vanilla extract

4 tablespoons demerara sugar

4 ramekins, 150 ml each

SERVES 4

A slightly healthier and much quicker version of the traditional crème brûlée, this can be made with fresh, ripe cherries or plums.

Preheat the grill to hot.

Put the cherries in a saucepan with 100 ml water. Cook over high heat until simmering, then lower the heat and simmer gently until the cherries have slightly softened, 5–7 minutes. Remove the pan from the heat.

Put the cream or crème fraîche, fromage frais and vanilla extract in a bowl and mix well. Divide the cherries between the ramekins. Spoon the cream mixture over the fruit, then top with 1 tablespoon of the demerara sugar.

Put the ramekins under the preheated grill until the sugar melts and begins to caramelize. Remove from the heat and serve immediately.

Variation If you are making this dessert for a special occasion, soak the cherries in 2–3 tablespoons kirsch or cherry brandy before topping with the cream mixture. If you prefer a cold pudding, put the brûlées in the fridge to chill. This will make the sugar set, making it even crunchier.

Ready-made filo pastry works well here, and it doesn't matter what it looks like when it goes into the oven. When it's baked and dusted with icing sugar, your strudel will taste and look sensational. Choose slightly tart, well-flavoured apples.

apple strudel

9 amaretti biscuits (50 g)

200 g filo pastry
(thawed if frozen)

50 g unsalted butter, melted

4 medium apples (800 g), peeled,
cored and sliced

70 g caster sugar

1½ teaspoons ground cinnamon

2 tablespoons raisins, flaked
almonds or dried blueberries

icing sugar, for dusting

ice cream or yoghurt, to serve

a large baking sheet, greased

SERVES 6

Preheat the oven to 200°C (400°F) Gas 6.

Put the amaretti biscuits in a plastic bag and crush with a rolling pin.

Arrange the filo pastry in overlapping sheets to make a rectangle about 55 x 70 cm. You should have several layers of pastry overlapping. Using a pastry brush, lightly brush about half the melted butter over the pastry. Sprinkle the amaretti crumbs on top, then add the apple slices, leaving a clear border of about 5 cm all around the edges. Sprinkle with the sugar and cinnamon, then add the raisins, almonds or blueberries.

To roll up the strudel, first fold over the pastry borders along the two short sides, then fold over the pastry border along one long side. Roll up the strudel from this side, and don't worry if the pastry splits and the filling falls out, just push it all back together with your hands. Transfer the strudel to the prepared baking sheet with the help of a couple of spatulas, if necessary. If the strudel is too big for the baking sheet you may have to curve it into a horseshoe. Brush all over with the rest of the melted butter.

Bake in the preheated oven for 35 minutes, or until golden brown. Remove from the oven and dust with icing sugar. Cut into thick slices and eat warm or at room temperature with ice cream or yoghurt.

A family favourite in French homes, this is the pudding to make for anyone who likes custard and sweet summer berries. The optional drizzle of rum at the end is strictly for the adults. You can also use ground almonds instead of the flour.

cherry clafoutis

450 ml milk

1 vanilla pod, cut lengthways

3 eggs

a pinch of salt

5 tablespoons caster sugar, plus extra for dredging

4 tablespoons plain flour

675 g fresh or frozen cherries

50 g unsalted butter, chilled and diced

a little dark rum (optional)

a medium, shallow baking dish

SERVES 4

Preheat the oven to 220°C (425°F) Gas 7.

Heat the milk and seeds scraped from the vanilla pod to blood temperature – you should be able to hold a finger in the liquid and count to ten without any pain.

Whisk the eggs lightly with the salt and sugar until pale, then whisk in the flour. Pour in the warmed milk, stirring to mix. Scatter the cherries in the baking dish and pour the batter over them. Dot with pieces of butter and bake in the preheated oven for about 25–30 minutes or until the batter is puffed and set around the cherries.

Remove from the oven and sprinkle with rum, if using, and liberally dredge with sugar before serving warm.

Everybody loves pavlova – adults and children alike. Raspberries are delicious with hazelnut and chocolate, but cherries and strawberries would also work well. Keep the cooled meringue in an airtight box until ready to use. You can make this up to one day ahead.

hazelnut and raspberry pavlova with hot chocolate sauce

4 large egg whites

a pinch of sea salt

225 g caster sugar, plus a little extra, to taste

1 teaspoon cornflour

1 teaspoon vanilla extract

1 teaspoon wine vinegar

100 g toasted chopped hazelnuts, plus extra for sprinkling

250 g raspberries, fresh or frozen and thawed

HOT CHOCOLATE SAUCE AND WHIPPED CREAM

200 g dark chocolate, chopped

650 ml double cream

50 g caster sugar, plus 1 tablespoon extra

30 g unsalted butter

a baking sheet, lined with non-stick baking parchment

SERVES 6

Preheat the oven to 140°C (275°F) Gas 1. Mark the lined baking sheet with a 25-cm circle.

Put the egg whites and salt in a bowl and whisk until very stiff. Gradually whisk in the sugar, a large spoonful at a time, making sure the meringue is 'bouncily' stiff before adding the next spoonful. Whisk the cornflour, vanilla extract and vinegar into the meringue. Fold in the hazelnuts.

Spoon the meringue into the circle on the baking sheet right to the edges, making it as rough as you like, but not too shallow. Make a slight dip in the centre.

Bake in the preheated oven for about 45 minutes until just beginning to turn the palest brown. Turn off the oven and leave to cool slowly still in the oven.

To make the hot chocolate sauce, put the chocolate, 200 ml of the cream, the sugar and butter in a saucepan. Stir until melted. Pour into a jug and keep it warm. Put the 1 tablespoon sugar and remaining cream in a bowl and whip until soft peaks form.

Carefully peel the baking parchment from the pavlova and set it on a serving dish. Dollop the cream generously on top and sprinkle with the raspberries. Trail the hot chocolate sauce over the top. Serve immediately.

Chocolate, butter, eggs and sugar; who needs flour? This is child's play to make and is best when made in advance – ideal for entertaining. It's supposed to be crumbly and almost raw in the middle, so if you're nervous about baking in public, this is the pudding for you because it always looks good. It is also the perfect after-dinner cake, rich and satisfying, and a nice companion when lingering over coffee after dinner.

flourless chocolate cake

200 g best-quality plain chocolate, broken into pieces

175 g unsalted butter, cubed

5 large eggs, separated

140 g caster sugar

raspberries, to serve (optional)

cream, to serve (optional)

a non-stick springform cake tin, 24 cm in diameter

SERVES 6–8

Preheat the oven to 180°C (350°F) Gas 4.

Put the chocolate and butter in a heatproof bowl set over a pan of simmering water and leave for several minutes until melted, then remove from the pan and leave to cool slightly.

Put the egg yolks and all but 2 tablespoons of the sugar in a large bowl. Beat vigorously until pale and fluffy, about 5 minutes. Set aside.

Put the egg whites in another bowl and beat on high until firm. Add the remaining 2 tablespoons sugar and continue beating until stiff peaks form. Set aside.

Stir the chocolate mixture into the egg yolk mixture and blend well. Add a third of the beaten whites and mix well until there are no white streaks. Carefully fold in the remaining whites, using a rubber spatula, until there are no white streaks. Pour into the cake tin and set it on a baking sheet.

Bake in the preheated oven until crisp around the edges, but still jiggly and almost raw looking in the very middle, 20–30 minutes. Leave to cool slightly, then run a knife around the inside edge of the tin to loosen and remove the outer ring. Serve at room temperature with raspberries and cream, if you like.

fruity carrot cake

100 ml sunflower oil

120 g light muscovado sugar

1 egg, beaten

3 egg whites

175 g carrots,
peeled and coarsely grated

1 cooking apple, about 175 g,
peeled, cored and grated

225 g sultanas

100 g prunes, chopped

50 g dried apricots, chopped

75 g dried blueberries or
sour cherries

1 teaspoon ground cinnamon

1 teaspoon baking powder

300 g wholemeal stoneground
plain flour

50 g self-raising flour

2 teaspoons demerara sugar

*a deep cake tin, 20.5 cm in diameter,
greased and lined with
greaseproof paper*

MAKES 12 SLICES

This delicious, moist cake is packed full of fruits – from prunes and dried apricots to grated fresh apple. Treat yourself to a slice with a mid-afternoon cup of tea, or pop a little portion in the children's lunchboxes.

Preheat the oven to 170°C (325°F) Gas 3.

Pour the oil into a large bowl, add the sugar and beat until smooth and free from lumps. Beat in the whole egg and the egg whites, a little at a time. Add the carrot, apple and dried fruit and stir well.

Sift the cinnamon, baking powder and flours into the mixture, adding any bran left in the sieve to the bowl. Stir gently until incorporated. Do not over-mix. Spoon the mixture into the prepared cake tin. Level the top with a spatula or round-bladed knife, then sprinkle the top with the demerara sugar.

Bake in the preheated oven for 1¼ hours, or until a skewer inserted into the centre comes out clean. Remove from the oven and leave to cool in the tin before turning out. Store in an airtight container for up to 1 week.

A classic Victoria sandwich filled with cream and fresh fruit makes a wonderful centrepiece for a traditional afternoon tea. Make it in the summer when strawberries are in season and at their juicy and fragrant best.

victoria sandwich
with strawberries and cream

180 g unsalted butter, at room temperature

180 g caster sugar

3 eggs

180 g self-raising flour

3½ tablespoons good-quality strawberry jam

140 g strawberries, hulled and halved or quartered, depending on size

120 ml whipping cream

icing sugar, for dusting

two 20-cm sandwich tins, greased and base-lined with greaseproof paper

SERVES 6–8

Preheat the oven to 180°C (350°F) Gas 4.

Beat together the butter and caster sugar in a large bowl until pale and fluffy. Beat in the eggs one at a time. Sift the flour into the mixture and fold in until thoroughly combined.

Spoon the cake mixture into the prepared tins and spread out evenly using the back of the spoon. Bake in the preheated oven for 20–25 minutes until golden brown and the sponge springs back when pressed gently with the tips of your fingers. Turn out the cakes onto a wire rack, gently peel off the lining paper and leave to cool completely.

Slice a thin sliver off the top of one of the cakes to create a flat surface. Spread the strawberry jam over the surface and top with the strawberries. Whip the cream until it stands in soft peaks, then spread on top of the strawberries. Top with the second cake, press down gently and dust with icing sugar.

oat and chocolate cookies

250 g butter, softened

50 g unrefined caster sugar

115 g light brown sugar

115 g plain chocolate chips

175 g oats

200 g self-raising flour

MAKES 15–20

These much-loved cookies will go down a treat with hungry children when they come home from school.

Preheat the oven to 180°C (350°F) Gas 4.

Beat the butter and sugars together until pale and creamy. Stir in the chocolate chips and oats. Add the flour and mix well.

Using your hands, form the mixture into 15–20 small balls. Flatten slightly with your palms and place them on a baking sheet, allowing room for growth. Bake in the preheated oven for 15–20 minutes. Transfer to a wire rack to cool, then store in an airtight container.

pumpkin seed cookies

200 g self-raising flour

125 g butter, diced

125 g light muscovado sugar

1 egg, beaten

75 g pumpkin seeds

MAKES 20

Seeds contain lots of nutrients that are an important part of a good diet. A great way to feed them to your family is to hide them in these tasty cookies.

Preheat the oven to 180°C (350°F) Gas 4.

Put the flour, butter and sugar in a bowl and mix with a fork until the mixture resembles breadcrumbs. Add the egg and seeds, mix again and form into a ball.

Lightly flour a work surface and use your hands to roll the dough into a sausage shape about 20 cm long. Cut into 20 slices and place on a non-stick or greased baking sheet. Bake in the preheated oven for 12–15 minutes. Transfer to a wire rack to cool, then store in an airtight container.

Kids will love to help you make these gingerbread people. Look out for cookie cutters in the shape of a princess, teddy bear, Father Christmas or any other favourite character.

gingerbread people

350 g self-raising flour

a pinch of salt

1 tablespoon ground ginger

200 g caster sugar

115 g unsalted butter

85 g golden syrup

1 large egg, beaten

TO DECORATE

raisins

edible silver balls

coloured chocolate buttons

2 or more baking sheets, greased

shaped cookie cutters

MAKES ABOUT 14 FIGURES

Preheat the oven to 160°C (325°F) Gas 3.

Sift the flour, salt and ground ginger into a large bowl. Add the sugar and mix in with a wooden spoon. Make a hollow in the centre.

Put the butter and syrup in a small saucepan. Heat very gently until melted – don't let the mixture become hot. Carefully pour into the hollow in the flour mixture. Pour the egg into the hollow on top of the melted mixture. Mix all the ingredients with a wooden spoon. As soon as the dough starts to come together, push it together into a ball. If it is too hot to handle, wait for it to cool.

Turn the dough out onto a work surface lightly dusted with flour. Gently roll out the dough to a large rectangle about 4 mm thick. Cut out figures with the cookie cutters, then transfer them to the prepared baking sheets, allowing room for growth. Gather the trimmings into a ball, then roll out and cut more figures as before.

Decorate the figures with raisins, silver balls or chocolate buttons. Bake in the preheated oven for about 15 minutes until golden brown. Watch them carefully, because they can quickly burn.

Remove from the oven and leave to cool on the sheets for 5 minutes. When the figures are firm, transfer to a wire rack. Cool completely and store in an airtight container for up to 1 week.

nutty chocolate and marshmallow on toast

2 thick slices of white bread

2 tablespoons single cream

15 g plain chocolate, grated or shaved, or good-quality plain chocolate chips

15 g pecan nuts

25 g mini-marshmallows

SERVES 2

Sinfully sweet and sticky, this toast is the ultimate in instant comfort food. It's lacking sophistication by anyone's standards, but it makes a luscious treat when you're feeling blue and need a no-effort pick-me-up.

Preheat the grill to medium.

Toast the bread on one side under the preheated grill, then flip over. Pour the cream over the untoasted side, sprinkle with the grated or shaved chocolate, nuts and marshmallows and grill until golden and bubbling. Eat with caution: the topping will be very hot!

Note This is definitely a recipe for those with a sweet tooth. You can use any type of white bread – a classic square white loaf, a white bloomer or several slices of white baguette cut diagonally. However, don't be tempted to try it with a sweet bread such as brioche or panettone – there's only so much sugar you should eat at once!

DRINKS

chilled lemongrass tisane

1–2 red chillies,
deseeded and sliced

2–4 lemongrass stalks,
outer leaves discarded,
inner section finely sliced

5 cm fresh ginger,
peeled and sliced

50 g caster sugar

freshly squeezed juice of 2 lemons

mint leaves and ice cubes, to serve

SERVES 4

Tisane is the French word for an infusion of herbs, flowers or other aromatics. This is an unusual, deliciously spicy version, which is chilled down to make a great contrast between hot and cold.

Put the chilli into a heatproof jug with the lemongrass, ginger and sugar, then add 1 litre boiling water and the lemon juice and stir to dissolve the sugar. Leave to infuse until cold.

Strain the cooled liquid and chill for at least 30 minutes. Serve in tall glasses with mint leaves and ice cubes.

orange and apple refresher

2 large oranges, peeled

2 Granny Smith apples

3 cm fresh ginger, peeled

ice cubes, to serve

a juicing machine

SERVES 2

This is the kind of zingy pick-me-up you need first thing in the morning to get you off to a great start.

Push the oranges, apples and ginger through the juicer. Half-fill 2 tall glasses with ice cubes, pour the juice over the top and serve.

This utterly delicious juice combo is a super-healthy way to start the day – kiwi fruit contains large amounts of vitamin C. If you're feeling brave, add a little watercress or rocket for a green, peppery hit. Juices and smoothies taste much better if the fruit is only just ripe (or even a little underripe); if too ripe, the taste will be dull. Transform this into a yoghurt smoothie in a blender, in which case it will serve two.

pear, apple and kiwi fruit juice with ginger

1 not-too-ripe pear

1 apple

2 not-too-ripe kiwi fruit

2.5 cm fresh ginger, peeled and coarsely chopped

SERVES 1

Juicer method Peel and core the pear and apple and cut into 6 wedges each. Peel and quarter the kiwi fruit. Put the pear through the juicer first, followed by the ginger, kiwi fruit and finally the apple. Stir well before serving, because it can separate. Drink as soon as possible and just feel those vitamins coursing through your body!

Blender smoothie Put all the prepared fruits and ginger in a blender with 150 ml natural yoghurt. Blend until smooth, adding a squeeze of lemon juice or a little salt to taste.

passion fruit and papaya blitz

1 orange

3 ice cubes

1 ripe papaya

2 passion fruit, halved

SERVES 1

A refreshing taste of the exotic for any time of day, but especially good on a hot summer's afternoon.

Squeeze the juice from the orange into a blender, adding the pulp from the citrus squeezer, together with the ice cubes. Halve the papaya, discard the seeds and scoop the flesh into the blender using a spoon. Blend until smooth, then stir in the seeds from the passion fruit. Mix briefly and serve in a glass.

strawberry shake

A filling smoothie to whip up for breakfast before you rush out the door and face the day.

3 ice cubes

4 tablespoons skimmed milk

4 tablespoons low-fat natural or strawberry yoghurt

125 g strawberries, hulled and chopped

½ banana, sliced

½ teaspoon vanilla extract

1 tablespoon clear honey

SERVES 1

Put all the ingredients in a blender and process until smooth. Pour into a glass and serve.

mango, raspberry and orange smoothie

This is a great accompaniment to a couple of slices of wholegrain toast, a banana or a bowl of cereal.

1 large orange

½ mango, peeled, stoned and chopped

75 g fresh or frozen raspberries

3 ice cubes (if using fresh berries)

SERVES 1

Squeeze the juice from the orange and pour into a blender, adding the pulp from the citrus squeezer. Add the chopped mango, raspberries and ice cubes, if using, and blend until smooth. Pour into a glass and serve.

pussyfoot

Pussyfoot is one of the best non-alcoholic drinks around, and greatly appreciated by designated drivers and pregnant women. It is very refreshing, thanks to the mellowing effect of the grenadine (sweet pomegranate syrup). Make sure the juices are freshly squeezed – carton juice just will not do. Leave out the egg yolk if there's any risk involved – it won't matter greatly, you can always add a tablespoon of cream.

50 ml freshly squeezed orange juice

25 ml freshly squeezed lemon juice

25 ml freshly squeezed lime juice

1–2 tablespoons grenadine

1 free-range egg yolk (optional)

ice cubes

SERVES 1

Pour the orange, lemon and lime juices, grenadine and optional egg yolk into a cocktail shaker half-filled with ice cubes. Shake well and strain into a glass filled with more ice cubes.

Variation Add a dash of sparkling water or lemonade for bit of festive fizz.

home-made fresh lemonade

Fresh lemonade is simple to make, and if you keep the lemony syrup in the fridge, you have an almost instant drink to dilute with either chilled sparkling mineral water or soda water on a sweltering day.

finely grated zest and freshly squeezed juice of 6 large, juicy, unwaxed lemons

180 g sugar

sparkling mineral water or soda water, chilled, to dilute

TO SERVE

ice cubes

fresh lemon slices

fresh mint sprigs

SERVES 6–8

Put the lemon zest, sugar and 625 ml water in a non-aluminium saucepan and bring slowly to a simmer, stirring to dissolve the sugar. As soon as the sugar has dissolved and the syrup begins to bubble, take it off the heat. Half cover and leave until cold.

Squeeze the lemons and add the juice to the cold syrup. Strain into a bowl or jug, cover and chill.

Serve in a glass jug with ice cubes, fresh lemon slices and sprigs of mint, diluted with chilled sparkling mineral water or soda water on a ratio of about 1 part syrup to 1 part water.

Variation Add a small pinch of saffron threads to the warm syrup when you take it off the heat.

pear and ginger juice

350 g ripe pears, peeled, cored
and chopped

1 large orange, peeled and
separated into segments

2 cm fresh ginger, chopped

2 tablespoons crushed ice, to serve
(optional)

SERVES 2

Pear is very gentle on the digestive system and ginger is an effective remedy against nausea and travel sickness, so this is a great drink to take on journeys or to give to your child after a stomach upset.

Push the pears, orange and ginger through a juicer. Put 1 tablespoon crushed ice, if using, in each of 2 tall glasses, pour the juice over the top and serve.

apple and carrot juice

3 medium carrots, chopped

2 apples, peeled, cored
and chopped

2 tablespoons crushed ice, to serve
(optional)

SERVES 2

This is high in soluble fibre, which is necessary for a healthy digestive system, and full of immune-boosting antioxidants.

Push the carrot and apple pieces through a juicer. Put 1 tablespoon crushed ice, if using, in each of 2 tall glasses, pour the juice over the top and serve.

iced ginger tea

50 g fresh ginger,
peeled and finely sliced

4 tea bags (preferably Indian tea)

2 limes, sliced

ice cubes, to serve

lemonade, to serve

SERVES 6

When making iced tea, it's best to add the tea bags to cold water rather than boiling water in order to avoid the unpleasant scum that can appear on the surface. So boil the water, then leave it to cool before adding the tea.

Put the sliced ginger into a large jug, pour over 1 litre boiling water and leave until cold. Add the tea bags and chill for 1 hour.

Strain the tea into a clean jug, add the slices of lime and ice cubes, then top up with lemonade.

iced lemon coffee

500 ml freshly brewed
espresso coffee

caster sugar, to taste

ice cubes, to serve

1 tablespoon freshly squeezed
lemon juice

6 twists of lemon zest, to serve

SERVES 6

Iced lemon coffee can be just as refreshing as iced lemon tea on a hot day. It may sound a little strange, but it's very thirst-quenching.

Pour the coffee into a large jug, add sugar to taste and stir until dissolved. Leave to cool, then chill until very cold.

Half-fill 6 glasses with ice cubes. Add the lemon juice to the coffee, then pour into the glasses and serve with a twist of lemon zest.

moroccan mint tea

1½ heaped tablespoons green
tea leaves

a handful of fresh mint leaves
(not spearmint)

150–180 g sugar, or to taste

SERVES 6

Mint tea is very soothing after a spicy meal. Don't use spearmint – it will taste like mouthwash.

Heat a teapot with just-boiled water. Tip out the water, add the tea leaves and pour a little boiling water over them just to moisten. Swirl around, then quickly pour the water out again, taking care not to lose any leaves. Add a good handful of fresh mint (the sugar is traditionally added at this stage, but leave it out or serve it later). Pour about 1 litre boiling water over the mint and moistened tea leaves. Put on the lid and leave to infuse for 5–8 minutes. Pour into warmed glasses and top with a few extra mint leaves. Hand the sugar around separately.

real hot chocolate

30 g plain chocolate,
finely chopped

1 teaspoon caster sugar

200 ml milk

TO SERVE (OPTIONAL)

whipped cream

mini-marshmallows

SERVES 1

Not a packet mix but the real thing – plain chocolate, milk and a dash of sugar, plus whipped cream and mini-marshmallows if you really want to have fun.

Put the chocolate, sugar and milk in a small saucepan. Heat up the milk until it is almost boiling. Stir occasionally with a wooden spoon to help the chocolate melt.

Remove the saucepan from the heat and put onto a heatproof surface. Using a rotary whisk, beat the milk until it is very smooth and foaming. Carefully pour the hot chocolate into a mug. Top with a swirl of cream (from a can, or whip some cream in a bowl with the rotary whisk) and sprinkle with a few mini-marshmallows, if using.

index

credits